MW00478712

THE UNITED STATES MARINE CORPS

Casemate Short History

THE UNITED STATES MARINE CORPS

THE EXPEDITIONARY FORCE AT WAR

Paul Westermeyer

CASEMATE

Philadelphia & Oxford

Published in United States of America and
the Great Britain in 2019 by
CASEMATE PUBLISHERS
1950 Lawrence Road, Havertown, PA 19083, USA
The Old Music Hall, 106–108 Cowley Road, Oxford OX4 1JE, UK

Hardback Edition: ISBN 978-1-61200-693-2
Digital Edition: ISBN 978-1-61200-694-9 (epub)

A CIP record for this book is available from the British Library

The views expressed in this book are those of the author and do not
necessarily reflect the official policy or views of any U.S. Government
organization.

Printed in the Czech Republic by FINIDR s.r.o.

Typeset in India for Casemate Publishing Services.
ww.casematepublishingservices.com

For a complete list of Casemate titles, please contact:

CASEMATE PUBLISHERS (US)
Telephone (610) 853-9131
Fax (610) 853-9146
Email: casemate@casematepublishers.com
www.casematepublishers.com

CASEMATE PUBLISHERS (UK)
Telephone (01865) 241249
Email: casemate-uk@casematepublishers.co.uk
www.casematepublishers.co.uk

CONTENTS

INTRODUCTION

'E isn't one o' the reg'lar Line, nor 'e isn't one of the crew.
'E's a kind of a giddy harumfrodite—soldier an' sailor too!

Rudyard Kipling, "Soldier an' Sailor Too" (1893)

From modest beginnings in the American Revolution to one of the world's most powerful combined-arms teams, the United States Marine Corps has served the United States. The Marine Corps is a somewhat unique military force, no other force of Marines is as large, nor as diverse in its style of arms. Today's Marine Corps includes armor, artillery, engineers, cyber warfare, and aviation amongst its capabilities, while remaining true to its slogan that every Marine is a rifleman.

It could be said that the Marine Corps is a cult that worships the idea of being a Marine, but that begs the question: What is a Marine?

Kipling's answer is fun and succinct but leaves many questions, especially for a modern military force. The United States has an Army, a Navy, and an Air Force, and each of those services has a fairly intuitive mission. The Marine Corps' mission is far less obvious, and indeed, paraphrasing General Victor Krulak, when push comes to shove, the United States does not need a Marine Corps but has decided it wants one. So chosen, and within the defense establishment of the United States, the Marine Corps has filled several distinct roles but the most enduring is as America's premier expeditionary force.

The Marine Corps was born as an accoutrement to the most complicated piece of military and transportation technology of its day, the fully rigged man-of-war. These large, complex vessels were startlingly advanced for their time, as their primary power came from non-human sources. They moved by harnessing the winds and currents, and they projected power mostly through chemistry, as the explosive characteristics of gunpowder sent the shot from their massive broadside batteries of cannon. It is difficult to recall today, following two centuries of rapid technological development, how marvelous the tall ships really were. But while they utilized nonhuman sources of energy to a greater extent than ever before, they still required large numbers of men to operate. Traditionally, sailors were men without nations, and so the emerging nation states employed marines in order to maintain order on the vessels, and to provide these formidable weapons of war with the ability to project power ashore.

The United States Marine Corps originally played this role, emulating the Royal Marines as well as the older Spanish and Dutch marines. In the Quasi-War with France, the Barbary Wars, and the War of 1812 the United States Marine Corps fulfilled this traditional task. Marines fought in ship actions as musket men and with boarding parties in engagements such as the famed USS *Constitution* versus HMS *Guerriere* duel as well as acting as landing parties such as the action at Farjado Bay, Puerto Rico in 1824. This initial, traditional role as naval infantry lasted through the American Civil War, when changes in naval technology and ordnance, as well as cultural changes in the world's navies eliminated the need for this form of naval infantry.

When technology revolutionized naval warfare in the late 19th century, the Marine Corps transformed, slowly, into an expeditionary force capable of projecting American power abroad. Marines specialized in amphibious warfare, preparing to seize and defend advanced naval bases and acting as tools of the State Department in foreign lands. As colonial forces,

The action between USS Constitution *and HMS* Guerriere, *August 19, 1812, was one of the most famous naval actions of the War of 1812. Marines fought fiercely aboard the USS* Constitution *as they did on all U.S. naval vessels during the war. (Painting by Michel Felice Corne)*

Marines advanced American interests in Haiti, the Dominican Republic, Panama, Nicaragua, China, the Philippines, and Cuba, suppressing revolutions and training indigenous forces.

However, the Corps' primary focus was on amphibious assaults and projecting power ashore, training to seize and hold advanced naval bases in support of the fleet. Guantanamo Bay during the 1898 Spanish–American War was first example of this role, but Marines refined and perfected the techniques through World War I, and World War II. In World War I, Marines reinforced the American Expeditionary Force, proving that they were a modern, elite military group capable of standing up to the best military forces in the world. Following the war, and the belief many had that assaulting heavily defended beaches was a fool's errand, the Marine Corps studied the failed allied landing at Gallipoli and developed techniques for successful amphibious assaults.

These techniques were justified during World War II, when the Marines used them to seize many heavily defended islands in the Pacific. The United States Army conducted even more amphibious landings during World War II, in both the Pacific and European theaters, but all of their assaults were conducted using the techniques and doctrines developed by the Marine Corps between the wars.

Following World War II the Marine Corps adjusted to the nuclear age, developing another set of amphibious warfare doctrines that took into account the dangers that future fleets would face. The Corps developed new doctrines and force structures for expeditionary warfare to respond to threats to American interests globally, whether it was the encroachment of communism during the Cold War or the threat of Islamic terrorism in the modern age.

The Corps' most recent form of expeditionary force is the Marine Air Ground Task Force, permanently constituted combined-arms forces paired with naval task forces and kept on station, providing the nation with on-the-spot options when a crisis occurs across the globe. The Corps has also returned to its old mission of counterinsurgency, providing aid and support to allied nations to promote stability. Marine officers also now serve in many of the highest positions of the Department of Defense. The Marine Corps today is a mature, elite fighting force that other nations' armed services judge themselves against.

From the Halls of Montezuma
To the shores of Tripoli;
We fight our country's battles
In the air, on land, and sea;
First to fight for right and freedom
And to keep our honor clean;
We are proud to claim the title
Of United States Marine.

Our flag's unfurled to every breeze
From dawn to setting sun;
We have fought in every clime and place

Where we could take a gun;
In the snow of far-off Northern lands
And in sunny tropic scenes,
You will find us always on the job
The United States Marines.

Here's health to you and to our Corps
Which we are proud to serve;
In many a strife we've fought for life
And never lost our nerve.
If the Army and the Navy
Ever look on Heaven's scenes,
They will find the streets are guarded
By United States Marines.

—The Marine's Hymn

1775–1783	American War of Independence
November 10, 1775	Congress authorizes raising two battalions of Continental Marines
March 3–4, 1776	The Marines' first amphibious landing as Captain Samuel Nichols leads a battalion of Marines and sailors in the landings at Nassau in the Bahamas
1798–1800	Quasi-War with France
July 11, 1798	The Act of 11 July 1798, "Establishing and Organizing a Marine Corps," approved by President John Adams
1801–1805	First Barbary War
November 29, 1804–June 12, 1805	The Tripolitan port of Derne is seized by Lieutenant Presley N. O'Bannon, USMC, William Eaton, Midshipman George Mann, seven Marines, and several hundred mercenaries and Arab allies. Supported by U.S. Navy warships *Argus*, *Nautilus* and *Hornet* they hold the city against counterassaults until the war ends
1812–1815	The War of 1812
August 24, 1814	A Marine battalion fights alongside sailors in the battle of Bladensburg, the unsuccessful defense of Washington, D.C.
January 8, 1815	Marines fight in the defenses of New Orleans
1846–1848	Mexican–American War
July 7, 1846–January 13, 1847	Marines from the Pacific Squadron aid in the conquest of California
September 13, 1847	The battle of Chapultepec
October 16–18, 1859	Led by Lieutenant Israel Greene, Marines aid in the capture of the abolitionist John Ford during his abortive uprising at Harpers Ferry

1861–1865	The American Civil War
July 21, 1861	The battle of Bull Run
December 1864–January 1865	Marines participate in the amphibious campaign to seize Fort Fisher outside of Wilmington, N.C.
April–August 1898	The Spanish–American War
June 10–August 9, 1898	Marines land at Guantanamo Bay, establishing an advanced naval base for the U.S. Navy's blockade of Cuba
1899–1902	The Philippine Insurrection
1899–1901	The Boxer Rebellion in China
1899, 1909–1910, & 1912–13	Marine intervention in Nicaragua
1901–1904	Marine intervention in Panama
1906–1909, 1912, 1917	Marine intervention in Cuba
1914	Marine intervention in Mexico
1915–1934	Marine intervention in Haiti
1916–1924	Marine intervention in the Dominican Republic
1914–1918	World War I
June 1–26, 1918	The 5th and 6th Marines fight in the battle of Belleau Wood
July 18–22, 1918	The 4th Marine Brigade fights in the battle of Soissons
September 12–15, 1918	The 4th Marine Brigade fights in the battle of Battle of Saint-Mihiel
October 3–27, 1918	The 4th Marine Brigade fights in the battle of Blanc Mont
September 26–November 11, 1918	The 4th Marine Brigade fights in the Meuse-Argonne offensive

1939–1945	World War II
December 7, 1941	The Japanese attack on Pearl Harbor brings the United States into the War
August 7, 1942– February 9, 1943	The 1st Marine Division and the 1st Marine Air Wing fight the Guadalcanal Campaign
November– December 1943	The I Marine Amphibious Corps fights in the battle of Bougainville
November 20–23, 1943	The 2d Marines seizes the island of Tarawa from the Japanese
July 21– August 10, 1944	The 3d Marine Division and the 1st Marine Provisional Brigade help retake Guam from the Japanese
July 24– August 1, 1944	Marines of the V Amphibious Corps take Tinian from the Japanese
December 26, 1943–January 16, 1944	The 1st Marine Division fights the battle of Cape Gloucester
June 15–July 9, 1944	Marines of the V Amphibious Corps take Saipan.
September 15–November 27, 1944	The 1st Marine division takes Peleliu
February 19–March 26, 1945	Marines of the V Amphibious Corps fight the battle of Iwo Jima
April 1–June 22, 1945	Marines of the III Amphibious Corps fight the battle of Okinawa
1950–1953	The Korean War
August 4– September 18, 1950	The 1st Provisional Marine Brigade fights in the battle of the Pusan Perimeter
September 10–19, 1950	The 1st Marine Division lands at Inchon

November 27–December 13, 1950	The 1st Marine Division fights its way out of the Chosin Reservoir
October 1962	Cuban Missile Crisis
1955–1975	The Vietnam War
January 30–March 3, 1968	Marines fight in the battle of Hue
January 21–April 6, 1968	Marines fight in the siege of Khe Sanh Combat Base
October 23, 1983	A terrorist suicide truck bomb is detonated at the barracks of the 24th Marine Amphibious Unit in Beirut, Lebanon
1990–1991	The Gulf War
September 9, 2001	Terrorists attack the World Trade Center in New York and the Pentagon in Washington, D.C.
October 7, 2001–December 28, 2014	Operation *Enduring Freedom*, American campaign to remove the Taleban and al-Qaeda from Afghanistan
March 20, 2003–December 18, 2011	Operation *Iraqi Freedom*, American campaign to remove Saddam Hussein from power and stabilize Iraq
November 7–December 23, 2004	Marines take the city of Fallujah in Iraq from insurgents
2006–2009	The Anbar Awakening in Iraq
2009–2014	Marines fight a counterinsurgency campaign in Afghanistan's Helmand Province

CHAPTER 1

REVOLUTION AND FRIGATE NAVY, 1775–1858

On November 10, 1775, the date traditionally given for the origin of the Marine Corps, the Continental Congress ordered that "two Battalions of Marines be raised" for service as landing forces with the fleet. Serving on land and at sea, these first Marines distinguished themselves in a number of important operations, including their first amphibious raid into the Bahamas in March 1776.

"Resolved, That two Battalions of Marines be raised, consisting of one Colonel, two Lieutenant Colonels, two Majors, and other officers as usual in other regiments; and that they consist of an equal number of privates with other battalions; that particular care be taken, that no persons be appointed to office, or enlisted into said Battalions, but such as are good seamen, or so acquainted with maritime affairs as to be able to serve to advantage by sea when required; that they be enlisted and commissioned to serve for and during the present war between Great Britain and the colonies, unless dismissed by order of Congress: that they be distinguished by the names of the first and second battalions of American Marines, and that they be considered as part of the number which the continental Army before Boston is ordered to consist of.

Ordered, That a copy of the above be transmitted to the General."

—Second Continental Congress on November 10, 1775.

Following the Revolutionary War and the formal reestablishment of the Marine Corps on July 11, 1798, Marines saw action in the Quasi-War with France (1798–1800), landed in Santo Domingo (1800), and took part in many operations against the Barbary pirates along the "shores of Tripoli" (1801–1815). Marines participated in numerous naval operations during the War of 1812, as well as participating in the defense of Washington at Bladensburg, Maryland (1814) and with Andrew Jackson in the defeat of the British at New Orleans (1815).

In the early days of the **U.S. Navy and Marine Corps**, the relationship between the ships' Marine detachments and the sailors was often fraught with tension. Some naval officers used the Marines as they saw fit, there were no standard regulations, and quarrels between Marines and crew, and between Marine and Navy officers, were common. The Second Commandant of the Marine Corps, Lieutenant Colonel William W. Burrows, encouraged his officers to defend their own and the Corps' honor, even by dueling if necessary, as this letter demonstrates:

> On board the GANGES, about 12 mos. ago, Lt. Gale, was struck by an Officer of the Navy, the Capt. took no notice of the Business and Gale got no satisfaction on the Cruise; the moment he arrived he call'd the Lieut. out and shot him; afterwards Politeness was restor'd.

The Quasi-War with France was fought almost entirely at sea, and was primarily concerned with commerce and the seizure of American ships; it began on May 28, 1798. Marines served on ships of the newly created United States Navy which fought several battles against French ships, including the *Constellation*

In the days of the tall sailing ships, Marines served in all of the Navy's major boarding actions. This drawing depicts the capture of the French Privateer Sandwich *by armed Marines on the Sloop* Sally, *from the USS* Constitution. *(National Archives and Records Administration #532590)*

versus the *Insurgente* in 1779, and versus the *Vengeance* in 1780. The Marines of the *Constitution* seized the *Sandwich* from the harbor at Puerto Plata, Santo Domingo, then the raiders seized the local fort and spiked its guns.

The following is an extract of a letter from an officer (Marine Captain Daniel Carmick) on board the *Constitution* to a friend in Philadelphia on May 12, 1800.[*]

Captain [Silas] Talbot had put his plan into execution respecting the cutting out the ship [*Sandwich*]. I performed my part with very little trouble, the only disagreeable part of the business was being cooped up in a small vessel for 12 hours—for we fortunately took a small American vessel [*Sally*] that had been in the part a few days before, and was to return there in a short time. By this means it was easy to take the vessel by surprize; it put me in mind of the Wooden Horse at Troy. We all remained below until we received orders from the officer, the only one of us who remained on the deck of the sloop, whose business it was to lay us on board, which he did on the starboard bow. The men went on board like Devils and it was as much as the first lieutenant [Isaac Hull] and myself could do to prevent blood being spilt. I believe it was not half an hour after the ship was taken, that I had possession of the Fort and all the cannon spiked, and returned again on board the prize before they could get any succor from the city. I presume they were rather surprized when they found the cannon spiked; we had then possession of the harbour, we took our time to rig the ship, as she had her topmasts down and all her sails unbent. By 6 o'clock the lieutenant had everything in order and the men stationed at the cannon, ready with my marines to oppose all their force which we understood was about five hundred men—they sent several Flags of Truce, making different requests, to which we answered that he had only executed the orders of

---

[*] *Gazette of the United States* and *Philadelphia Daily Advertiser*, June 2, 1800.

our commander. On shore they were not ignorant, that it was impossible for us to get out until the land breeze came off, which you know is in the morning; he concluded we must have been pretty determined before we undertook the business, as we had no other alternative than to die or succeed—he however remained very quiet, and we came out in the morning and joined our commodore.

The night before we performed this business, in going to Porto Plate we were met at 12 o'clock at night by an English frigate [*Alarm*] who fired two shot and brought us too—we went on board and after examining us we proceeded; we suspected he was going on the same business we were upon; he will peep into the harbour La Plate today and find his plans frustrated. The English captain [Robert Rolles] informed us, that he was cruizing to intercept a French frigate arrived at St. Domingo from France, and was to proceed round to Cape Francois.

The Barbary Wars saw the Marine Corps acting as an expeditionary force in addition to its shipboard duties. The continuing depredations of the Barbary pirates drove the United States to naval force when paying them off was ineffective, beginning in 1801. The U.S. Navy's Mediterranean Squadron arrived on station in 1801 to protect American merchant ships, but had little success. Then, Tripolitan pirates captured the grounded frigate *Philadelphia*. In 1804, Lieutenant Stephan Decatur, USN, took 70 Marines and sailors into Tripoli harbor at night. They boarded the captured *Philadelphia*, overpowered the pirate crew, and burned the ship and returned to their own craft.

In 1805, William Eaton, an American soldier and diplomat, led a small group of Marines under Lieutenant Presley N. O'Bannon, along with the Pasha of Tripoli's deposed brother and an army of Arabs and Greek mercenaries, 600 miles across the North African desert from Egypt and captured Derna, Tripoli. This action was immortalized in the Marine Hymn, and was the first time the flag of the United States was raised over conquered foreign territory.

*The most famous of the early U.S. Navy frigates was "Old Ironsides,"
the USS* Constitution. *Marines served aboard it in all of its legendary
engagements. (Painting by Michele Felice Corne)*

During the War of 1812, Marine detachments served on nearly
all of the Navy's vessels. They fought on Lake Erie under Oliver
Perry and played an important role in the famous victories won
by the USS *Constitution* and the other legendary American
frigates. They shared in the defeats as well, three-fourths of the
Marines aboard the ill-fated *Chesapeake* were killed or wounded
during its duel with the *Shannon* on June 13, 1813.

Marines also fought in major land engagements war; a
detachment of Marines and sailors fought at the battle of
Bladensburg, holding the field after all other American troops
had fled. During December 1814 and January 1815, Marines
helped repulse the British at New Orleans.

In the Pacific, First Lieutenant John M. Gamble, serving on
Captain Porter's *Essex* in April 1813, was placed in command of
a captured British whaler which had been refitted as a 20-gun
man-of-war. Gamble proceeded to attack and capture another

British vessel, the first time a Marine officer ever commanded an American man-of-war in battle.

The decades following the War of 1812 saw the Marines protecting American interests around the world, in the Caribbean (1821–1822), the Falkland Islands (1832), Sumatra (1831–32), off the coast of West Africa (1820–61), and also close to home in the operations against the Seminole Indians in Florida (1836–42).

During the Mexican War (1846–48) Marines seized many enemy seaports on both the Gulf and Pacific coasts. While landing parties of Marines and sailors were seizing enemy ports along the coast, a battalion of Marines joined General Scott's

In 1820, **Commandant Colonel Archibald Henderson** was appointed the Fifth Commandant of the Marine Corps at the age of 37. Enthusiastic and aggressive, Henderson introduced higher standards for personal appearance, training, and discipline. He also pushed the Marine Band for performances throughout Washington, D.C., beginning the process which would lead eventually to its status as "The President's Own."

In 1836, Colonel Henderson volunteered the services of a regiment of Marines to aid the army in the Seminole Wars, which he formed by stripping all available detachments and posts throughout the Corps. On a note pinned to his officer door he wrote, "Gone to Florida to fight the Indians. Will be back when the war is over." The Marines campaigned in the southern swamps for several years. In 1837, Henderson was given command of a brigade composed of Marines and an Army regiment, and he was brevetted to brigadier general. After the war he returned to Washington and continued to lead the Corps.

Archibald Henderson served under nine Presidents during his 38-year tenure as commandant, earning him the title, "grand old man of the Corps."

army at Puebla and marched and fought all the way to the "Halls of Montezuma," Mexico City.

After the declaration of war in May 1846, Marines seized numerous enemy seaports, including Tampico and Alvarado. At times the separate Marine detachments from various ships made amphibious landings. At other times they landed jointly with sailors or Army units. Occasionally, all Marines in the squadron were formed into a battalion led by the squadron Marine officer.

Approaching Mexico City, a battalion of Marines provided the storming parties for General Quitman's division during the assault, silencing the enemy artillery battery. Marines and soldiers captured the stronghold of Chapultapec and Mexico

The New York, Pennsylvania, and South Carolina volunteers with the battalion of Marines advancing to the attack on the fortifications of Chapultepec. The capture of the fortress of Chapultepec served as the climax of the Mexican–American War. Marines serving alongside Army forces in General Winfield Scott's column helped to secure the stronghold. (Marine Corps Art Collection)

Many military forces are devoted to **ceremonial and security functions**. Marines might balk at the description, but the Corps has often served the nation in this way. The United States Marine Band has been known as the "President's Own" since 1801. The Marine Barracks in Washington, D.C. still provides Marines for ceremonial duties at the White House, as well as housing the U.S. Marine Drum and Bugle Corps, and the United States Marine Corps Silent Drill Platoon. These Marines perform sunset and evening parades at the Marine Barracks and the Marine Corps Memorial weekly during the summers. Marine Helicopter Squadron One (HMX-1) provides helicopter transportation to the President and since 1946 Marine Security Guard detachments have been stationed at American embassies, making the Marine blue dress uniform a visual reminder of America around the globe.

City, adding another line to the Marines' Hymn, "the Halls of Montezuma."

Prior to the war, the Pacific squadrons' orders were, upon determining "beyond a doubt" that war had been declared, to capture the ports of California. Commanded by Commodore John Drake Sloat, the squadron's ships operated out of store ships that provided naval supplies while they purchased food and obtained water from local ports of call in the Sandwich Islands and on the Pacific coast. While the Marines and sailors of the squadron awaited orders, a Marine, First Lieutenant Archibald H. Gillespie, was making his way across Mexico with secret orders from President James K. Polk. When war was declared, and Gillespie reached California, Marines landed along the coast, fighting several small engagements and aiding in the conquest of California.

Following the Mexican–American War, the Marines continued serving on naval vessels and in landing parties around the globe. In 1840, ships' detachments landed several times on the Fiji

The Marine Band's most famous director was John Phillips Sousa, who served in the band from 1868 to 1875, and directed it from 1880 to 1892, during which period it was the premier military band in the United States. (Beatty and Votteler lithograph)

Just before the Civil War, Marines serving in traditional roles on U.S. naval vessels carried out amphibious assaults as required by American foreign policy. One such event was the attack on the barrier forts near Canton, China, by the American squadron of Commodore James Armstrong, on November 21, 1856. This engraving depicts the landing of U.S. sailors and Marines from USS Portsmouth, Levant, *and steam frigate* San Jacinto. *USS* Portsmouth *and USS* Levant *are shown supporting the operation with gunfire. ("The Attack on the Barrier Forts near Canton, China" by J. H. Buffords, Boston Massachusetts, lithographer, after a sketch by A. Poinsett)*

Islands and the next year they went ashore in Samoa and the Gilbert Islands. Marines and sailors landed in Africa to suppress the slave trade and in Canton to protect Americans from a mob. They landed in Buenos Aires, in 1852, to protect American lives and property against a riot. Marines served in Commodore Perry's squadron when it journeyed to Japan and negotiated trade agreements with the reclusive kingdom in 1853 and 1854.

In 1856 Marines from the East India Squadron made several landings in Canton, China and attacked a series of barrier forts down river from the city. Spearheaded by approximately 50 Marines, the 287-man naval landing force defeated more than 400 Chinese and destroyed four forts within a few days.

CHAPTER 2

STEAM NAVY CIVIL WAR TO SPANISH–AMERICAN WAR, 1859–1899

> *"Visit the Navy-Yard, and behold a marine, such a man as an American government can make, or such as it can make a man with its black arts—a mere shadow and reminiscence of humanity, a man laid out alive and standing, and already, as one may say, buried under arms with funeral accompaniments…"*

Henry David Thoreau, "Civil Disobedience," 1854

In October 1859, Marines from the Washington Barracks were sent with Colonel Robert E. Lee to capture abolitionist leader, John Brown, who had seized the Federal arsenal at Harpers Ferry and was attempting to incite a slave revolt. Refusing to assault Brown and his men, a militia officer motioned to the Marines and said, "Let the mercenaries do it." First Lieutenant Israel Greene and 86 men from Marine Headquarters assaulted Harpers Ferry and captured him.

Marines served ashore and afloat in the Civil War (1861–1865). Although most Marine service was with the Navy, a battalion fought at Bull Run and other units saw action with the blockading squadrons and at Cape Hatteras, New Orleans, Charleston, and Fort Fisher.

As it had for decades, the Corps functioned as detachments on Navy vessels. Ships' detachments continued to serve as sharpshooters and landing parties while the Navy blockaded

ASSAULT OF THE NAVAL COLUMN ON THE NORTH-EAST SALIENT OF FORT FISHER.

The Marines formed the trained core of naval landing parties throughout the 19th century. During the assaults on Fort Fisher, Marines from the squadron fought alongside sailors in an assault on the fort, a precursor of the amphibious warfare that would become the Corps' primary function in the 20th century. This depiction of the assault of the naval column on Fort Fisher's Northeast Bastion was first published in 1884. (From Battles and Leaders of the Civil War, *1884)*

southern ports. But this left no spare Marines to serve with the Army. In July, 1861, a battalion of untrained recruits, which had spent the majority of their few short weeks as Marines marching from one point to another, fought at the first battle of Bull Run. When the rest of the Federal forces ran from the field, the Marines joined them.

Marines landed and assisted in capturing southern forts at Hatteras Inlet; Port Royal, South Carolina; St. Augustine, Florida; and Fort Fisher, North Carolina. In New Orleans in April 1862, Marine battalion Captain David Farragut's squadron took possession of the city. For heroism during the battle at Drewry's Bluff outside Richmond, Virginia, Corporal John F. Mackie was the first Marine to receive the Medal of Honor. Part of his citation reads:

On board the U.S.S. *Galena* in the attack on Fort Darling at Drewry's Bluff, James River, on May 15, 1862. As enemy

During the Civil War the Marine Corps, like the Army and Navy, increased dramatically in size. Marines were trained at the Marine Barracks at the Navy Yards in New York, Philadelphia, and Washington, D.C. A hastily raised battalion of new Marine recruits fought poorly at the first battle of Bull Run, after which Marines fought in their traditional roles on naval forces blockading the southern coasts. (Engraving of "The United States Marines and Marine Barracks at Washington," Harper's Weekly, June 1861)

shellfire raked the deck of his ship, Corporal Mackie fearlessly maintained his musket fire against the rifle pits along the shore and, when ordered to fill vacancies at guns caused by men wounded and killed in action, manned the weapon with skill and courage.

The last third of the 19th century saw Marines making numerous landings throughout the world, especially in the Orient and the Caribbean area. The increase in the size of naval guns, the advent of steam, and the increasing professionalism of the Navy reduced the need for the traditional Marine role. Marines continued to be kept busy as naval landing parties, and serving alongside naval gunners.

Many landings were made across the globe but they seldom required combat, the exception came in Korea in 1871.

In June, 1871 a diplomatic misunderstanding led to Korean forts firing on an American naval squadron. The squadron landed a naval brigade, built around a core of ships' Marine detachments, which advanced overland on the Salee River forts and captured them. Here is the Sujagi flag, captured at Fort McKee in the attacks on the Salee River forts, by Corporal Charles Brown of the USS Colorado *(left) and Private Hugh Purvis of the USS* Alaska *(middle). Both were awarded the Medal of Honor. Captain McLane Tilton, USMC, (right) commanded the Marines. This photograph was taken on the USS* Colorado. *(Official USMC photograph)*

Following attacks on American ships the American minister to China attempted to negotiate a treaty with the Korean officials. Two American naval vessels sailing up the Yom River were fired on by Korean forts. When the Koreans failed to apologize, a provisional battalion of Marines and sailors landed and captured three forts.

Protecting Americans citizens and property throughout the end of the 19th century, Marines made landings on Alexandria, Egypt, on the Isthmus of Panama, and on Haiti.

As the 20th century approached, thoughtful Marines had cause to be concerned for the future of their Corps. Founded during the American War of Independence almost as an afterthought, the Corps served throughout the 19th century in the traditional Marine role of ships' detachments—maintaining shipboard

When it was created at the close of the 18th century, **the Marine Corps was organized** as a battalion, with individual detachments aboard navy vessels as required and Marines divided into companies at the various Marine barracks.

This organization continued throughout the 19th century even as the Corps expanded, with ad hoc battalions being formed for service with the army in all of the major conflicts. At the close of the 19th century the 1st Marine Battalion was formed for the landing at Guantanamo Bay during the Spanish–American War.

At the start of the 20th century, the Corps was organized into the Advanced Base Force (the forerunner of the Fleet Marine Force), separate companies, ship detachments, and barracks garrisons. More and more often in the following decades Marines were organized into provisional battalions for service overseas, and the Advanced Base Force turned into a permanent battalion before becoming the Advanced Base Force Regiment.

During World War I, the Marine Corps was organized into permanent regiments which served as part of the Fleet Marine Force, a permanently constituted expeditionary force attached to the Atlantic and Pacific fleets of the Navy. The numbered companies, a holdover from the Corps' days of separate companies, were given letter designations based on which battalion they belonged to in the regiment, following Army unit nomenclature of the time. Ship detachments continued to serve aboard navy capital ships until the 1990s.

Marine aviation began with the Marine Aviation Company in the Advanced Base Force, and then deployed in World War I as the First Aeronautic Company and the 1st Marine Aviation Force. After the war Marine aviation was reorganized into squadrons.

When World War II came around the Marine Corps had been organized several times into provisional brigades as Marine regiments were reinforced with supporting arms. Now, the Corps formed permanently designated divisions for the Fleet Marine Force, fielding six of them by the end of the conflict. Marine aviation matched the regiments and divisions with air groups and air wings.

Following the war the Corps disbanded all but four of its divisions. In the 21st century the 1st, 2d and 3d Marine Divisions remain on active duty, while the 4th Marine Division comprises the Marine Corps reserve, the 1st, 2d, and 3d Marine Air Wings mirror the ground component, with the 4th Marine Air Wing comprised of reservists.

In the middle of the 20th century the Marine Corps adopted the Marine air-ground task force as its primary fighting formation, but traditional Marine regiments remain when the Corps deploys forces in support of land operations.

discipline, and providing trained soldiery for boarding and landing parties. In addition, the budget-conscious American government added naval yard security to the traditional duties of Marines in the Age of Sail. The early Corps performed these duties honorably, occasionally with distinction, and also often served ashore to augment the small United States Army, most notably in the Seminole Wars, the Mexican War, and the Civil War.

Despite the Corps' demonstrated usefulness, at the end of the 19th century obsolescence threatened. Naval technology and changing demographics were quickly rendering the Corps' traditional duties moot. The Corps' future as a combat organization was bleak; it seemed likely it would be absorbed by the Army or reduced to the ceremonial band in the capital and watchmen at various naval yards along the coasts.

Instead, over the next decades the Marine Corps transformed itself, increasing dramatically the professionalism of its officers and finding a *raison d'etre* as the nation's expeditionary force. The harsh realities of wind and sail had provided the need for Marines in the Age of Sail, and the technological necessities of the Age of Steam provided the same impetus for Marines. Navies required overseas bases in order to project their power, and the

In many ways the modern Marine Corps was born during the Spanish–American War, when a battalion of Marines seized Guantanamo Bay, Cuba, as an advanced naval base. This allowed the U.S. Navy to maintain a close, effective blockade of Cuba. Here, Lieutenant Herbert Draper raises the flag over the captured territory, the first raising of the American flag on Cuban soil during the war. (Official USMC photograph)

Corps would (occasionally over its own objections) take the mission of seizing and defending advanced naval bases.

The Spanish–American War illustrated this future when a battalion of Marines seized Guantanamo Bay as a forward base from which the Navy could blockade the island of Cuba. The Corps' success at Guantanamo compared favorably to the more haphazard embarkation and ship of the Army expedition, as did the deployment of Marines in the Far East as "colonial infantry." However, the Army's own increased professionalism and sense of purpose added another danger to the Corps. Army officers saw the volunteer regiments and state militias that comprised a large percentage of American ground forces up through the Spanish–American War as the primary cause for the chaos and unprofessionalism of mobilization in that conflict, and lobbied

After landing, the Marines fortified their position at Camp McCalla, adding four 3-inch naval cannons. On June 11, 1898, firing started on the camp, an attack that lasted 100 hours, during which the Spanish were driven off multiple times. In this image, Captain Francis H. Harrington stands in a fortified position which includes a 3-inch naval landing gun and Marine infantry at Camp McCalla. (Official USMC photograph)

to formalize the state forces into the "National Guard." This put the Corps' secondary purpose as an augmentation of American land forces at risk.

CHAPTER 3

THE CORPS COMES OF AGE, 1899–1919

Following the Spanish–American War (1898), in which Marines performed with valor in Cuba, Puerto Rico, Guam, and the Philippines, the Corps entered an era of expansion and professional development. It saw active service in the Philippine Insurrection (1899–1902), the Boxer Rebellion in China (1900), and in numerous other nations, including Nicaragua (1899, 1909–10, 1912–13), Panama (1901, 1902, 1903–04), the Dominican Republic (1903, 1904, 1916–24), Cuba (1906–09, 1912, 1917), Mexico (1914), and Haiti (1915–34).

The United States found itself the owner of the Philippines following the Spanish–American War. When the islands were not immediately granted their independence, the insurrection which had been brewing against Spain shifted focus to the Americans. A Marine battalion first arrived in the Philippines in May 1899 to protect the Cavite naval base. Later Marines assisted the Army in putting down the Moro insurrection in 1901, making several expeditions against the Moros. In January 1902, a detachment under the command of Major L. W. T. Waller finished an ill-fated march across Samar that has entered Marine legend. For years afterwards, when a veteran of the Samar patrol entered a Marine mess, a toast would be called by his fellow officers, "Stand, gentleman, he served on Samar." Even after the Moro

During the first half of the 20th century, the Marine Corps gained a reputation for adventurous service in exotic foreign lands. The Corps capitalized on this reputation in recruiting, looking to attract men who would enjoy travel. The reality of overseas service was seldom as glamorous as it was depicted in posters like this. (1917 recruiting poster)

insurrection was tamped down, Marines remained in the Cavite and Olangapo naval yards.

In the summer of 1900, the Boxer Rebellion occurred in China. Marines under the command of Captain John T. Meyers defended the American legation at Peking for three months. Edwin N. Conger, U.S. Minister to China, commended the Marines who defended the legations. "To our Marines fell the most difficult and dangerous portion of the defense by reason of our proximity to the great city wall and the main city gate.... The Marines acquitted themselves nobly." During the defense of the legation, Sergeant Major Dan Daly, one of only two Marines to earn two Medals of Honor, was awarded his first Medal of Honor for single-handedly defending his position against repeated attacks and inflicting around 200 casualties on the attacking Boxers.

"**Defining the Duties of the United States Marine Corps**," President Theodore Roosevelt
Executive Order No. 969, 3 C.F.R., November 12, 1908
In accordance with the power vested in me by section 1619, Revised Statutes of the United States, the following duties are assigned to the United States Marine Corps:

(1) To garrison the different navy yards and naval stations, both within and beyond the continental limits of the United States.
(2) To furnish the first line of the mobile defense of naval bases and naval stations beyond the continental limits of the United States.
(3) To man such naval defenses, and to aid in manning, if necessary, such other defenses, as may be erected for the defense of naval bases and naval stations beyond the continental limits of the United States.
(4) To garrison the Isthmian Canal Zone, Panama.
(5) To furnish such garrisons and expeditionary forces for duties beyond the seas as may be necessary in time of peace.

An ad hoc battalion of Marines, including then Lieutenant Smedley Butler (the other Marine who earned two Medals of Honor in his career), fought alongside Russian, British, German, Japanese, and United States soldiers in an international expeditionary force that made its way from the coast to the legations in Peking.

Throughout the first decade of the 20th century, ships' detachments of Marines landed to protect Americans and property on many shores, including Panama, Honduras, the Dominican Republic, and Beirut. In 1903, Marines served as guards for a United States diplomatic mission traveling to Abyssinia by camel caravan. They also served at new diplomatic stations in Cuba, Samoa, Midway, and Korea; travel around the globe became the norm for service in the Corps.

A brigade of the Corps served in the Army of Cuban Pacification from 1906 until 1909. They returned intermittently in the intervening years and since 1934, Marines have been stationed in Cuba to guard the large naval base at Guantanamo Bay.

In 1910 the Advance Base School was created in order to focus thinking on the unique problems of amphibious warfare and the Advance Base Force was created with its own supporting arms and kept ready for service with the fleet, the ancestor of today's Marine Air-Ground Task Force. The Advance Base Force landed at Vera Cruz in 1914 following the Tampico incident during the Mexican Revolution.

——— ———

Major General Smedley D. Butler served as a Marine Corps Officer from 1898 until 1931, participating in numerous campaigns and conflicts. He was already a combat veteran from the Philippine–American War when he was wounded during the legation relief expedition in China and later awarded the Brevet Medal for aiding another wounded officer to safety.

Recalling his time as a lieutenant in Asia, Butler said, "I selected an enormous Marine Corps emblem to be tattooed across my chest. It required several sittings and hurt me like the devil, but the finished product was worth the pain. I blazed triumphantly forth, a Marine from throat to waist. The emblem is still with me. Nothing on earth but skinning will remove it."

Butler went on to command Marines in Honduras, Nicaragua, and Haiti fighting the Banana Wars. He undertook a spy mission to Mexico City in 1914 and then commanded a battalion of Marines in the Vera Cruz landings, for which he was awarded his first Medal of Honor. In Haiti on November 17, 1915 he led his Marines in an assault on an insurgent stronghold, Fort Riviere, for which he was awarded his second Medal of Honor. Part of the citation reads:

> Following a concentrated drive, several different detachments of marines gradually closed in on the old French bastion fort in an effort to cut off all avenues of retreat for the Caco bandits. Reaching the fort on the southern side where there was a small opening in the wall, Major Butler gave the signal to attack and marines from the Fifteenth Company poured through the breach, engaged the Cacos in hand-to hand combat, took the bastion and crushed the Caco resistance.

Butler then commanded the 5th Marine Brigade in France during World War I and the Marine Corps Base Quantico. In the early 1920s he took a leave of absence from the Corps to serve as the Director of Public Safety in Philadelphia, fighting corruption and organized crime in the police and fire departments.

In the late 1920s he commanded the Marine Expeditionary Force in China. This was a modern, combined-arms force which included armor artillery and aircraft and was intended to monitor the increasing tensions between China and Japan. Butler retired from the Corps in 1931.

Following retirement Butler wrote a book, *War is a Racket* (1935), and unsuccessfully ran for Congress. When he passed away in 1940 he was the most decorated Marine at that time. He remains one of only two marines to have been awarded the Medal of Honor twice. Butler neatly summarizes his career:

I spent 33 years and four months in active military service and during that period I spent most of my time as a high class muscle man for Big Business, for Wall Street and the bankers. In short, I was a racketeer, a gangster for capitalism. I helped make Mexico and especially Tampico safe for American oil interests in 1914. I helped make Haiti and Cuba a decent place for the National City Bank boys to collect revenues in. I helped in the raping of half a dozen Central American republics for the benefit of Wall Street. I helped purify Nicaragua for the International Banking House of Brown Brothers in 1902–1912. I brought light to the Dominican Republic for the American sugar interests in 1916. I helped make Honduras right for the American fruit companies in 1903. In China in 1927 I helped see to it that Standard Oil went on its way unmolested. Looking back on it, I might have given Al Capone a few hints. The best he could do was to operate his racket in three districts. I operated on three continents.

Supporting United States policy in the Caribbean and South America, Marines were ordered to land in several Latin-American countries throughout the first half of the 20th century. Since these landings were often in relation to American business prospects, especially fruit companies, these are referred to as the "Banana Wars." Additionally, the strategic position of such islands as Cuba and Hispaniola threatened the Panama Canal, so the United States was determined to protect it. Political realities at home made it easier to employ the Navy and Marines as an arm of the State Department in these areas. The result was that Marines were found continually occupied in one or more extensive military interventions in Caribbean countries during this period.

As in Cuba and Panama, Marines assisted in stabilizing the Dominican Republic. In 1912 a regiment was sent to Santo

Fighting in the Banana Wars required the Marines to patrol in extremely difficult terrain and unusual conditions. In the jungle, rivers are arteries of communication. Here, Marines patrolling the Coco river in Nicaruagua in small boats pause for a break, circa 1929. (Coco River Patrol Collection [COLL/581] at the Archives Branch, Marine Corps History Division)

Domingo City but a landing became unnecessary. The Marines returned again and by 1916 an entire brigade was occupied in the Dominican Republic. Marines supported the American State Department policies, organized and trained a native constabulary, and continually combatted insurgents there until 1924.

Haiti closely paralleled her sister republic, a detachment of Marines landed in Haiti in 1914. During the next year Haitian revolutionists became more active, and a brigade of Marines was organized. Navy and Marine officers trained Haitian officials and supported road building, communications, education, and other public works. The Marines also organized and officered the gendarmerie, which was gradually transformed into an all-native Haitian force.

The Cacos were the primary Haitian insurgents. Despite tactical success against the Cacos, the Haitian insurgency was difficult to quell and Marines did not finally leave Haiti until 1934.

In Nicaragua, Marines intervention was also long and extensive. Starting in 1910 Marines intervened to protect American lives and property during Nicaraguan revolutions. The Marines again

Marines landing under fire at Santo Domingo City. Early 20th-century landings looked nothing like the combined-armed, sophisticated but bloody assaults of World War II. Although coming ashore from steamships, the Marines leapt over the gunnels of oared boats when they hit the beach, as Marines had for centuries before. (Records of the U.S. Marine Corps [Record Group 127], NARA)

The Marine Corps was quick to adapt to aviation as a means of fulfilling its primary missions. For Marines, the purpose of aviation was to support the Marine on the ground. In Nicaragua the Corps developed dive bombing and other close-air support techniques while using aircraft to maintain communications with far-flung outposts. Later, the Corps realized that defending advanced naval bases against amphibious attacks would require land-based aircraft capable of naval patrols, anti-submarine work, naval strike, and fighter interception. (National Air and Space Museum Poster Collection)

Gunnery Sergeant Dan Daly is a Marine Corps legend, and one of only two marines to be awarded two Medals of Honor. He fought in all of the Corps' major campaigns in the first half of the 20th century. It was in fights against the Haitian Cacos that he was awarded his second Medal of Honor:

> Gunnery Sergeant Daly was one of the company to leave Fort Liberte, Haiti, for a 6-day reconnaissance. After dark on the evening of 24 October, while crossing the river in a deep ravine, the detachment was suddenly fired upon from three sides by about 400 Cacos concealed in bushes about 100 yards from the fort. The Marine detachment fought its way forward to a good position, which it maintained during the night, although subjected to a continuous fire from the Cacos. At daybreak the Marines, in three squads, advanced in three different directions, surprising and scattering the Cacos in all directions. Gunnery Sergeant Daly fought with exceptional gallantry against heavy odds throughout this action.

landed in 1912 to guard the railroad, and patrolled extensively until the majority of the Marines withdrew in 1913. In 1925 civil war broke out, and by 1927, a Marine brigade was fighting the rebels. Marines created and officered the Guardia Nacional while fighting a counterinsurgency campaign against the rebels. By 1932, the Guardia was strong enough to fight on its own and the Marines pulled out of Nicaragua.

Many within the Marine Corps saw the Banana Wars as a distraction from the Corps' primary mission as the Navy's expeditionary force, prepared to seize and defend advanced naval bases. But the Corps developed techniques of counterinsurgency, as detailed in the 1940 *Small Wars Manual*, that served it for a long time. As well, nearly every senior marine leader, whether officer or NCO, served in the Banana Wars and honed their

Following the Spanish–American War, Marine service as the U.S. Navy's expeditionary force was increasing important and highlighted in recruiting materials, like this World War I-era recruiting poster, Join the U.S. Marine Corps—Soldiers of the Sea! *It depicts a Marine holding a Lewis machine gun and standing in the bow of a small boat. (Library of Congress Prints and Photographs Division)*

leadership skills there. When the Marines faced the Japanese on Guadalcanal, they had far more jungle-fighting experience then their opponents.

America's entry into World War I was an opportunity for the Corps to prove its increased professionalism, and its value as a

The Marine Corps earned the nickname "Devil Dog" during World War I. According to lore, it came from the use of "teufel hunde" by German soldiers to describe Marines fighting in WWI. This is unlikely. There are no records of the Germans using the phrase to describe Marines, and in German "devil dog" would be "Höllenhunde." Most likely the phrase, which appears in several sources a few months before Marines first saw action on the Western Front, was created by Marines on recruiting duty in New York. Regardless of the source, the Corps' performance during WWI more than justified the nickname. (Art Collection, National Museum of the Marine Corps)

military service, but there were significant difficulties. The Army was equally determined to prove it was a modern, professional organization on par with European armies. It was not eager to grant the Navy Department's land forces a chance to show it up. Organizationally, the Corps would have to field regiments and brigades to act on the Western Front and the Army questioned whether or not the Corps had any officers capable of commanding and staffing large land forces of that nature. And like the Army, the Marine Corps would be forced to expand rapidly, going from 10,397 officers and men in 1916 to 75,101 in 1918.

The Corps responded to these challenges with vigor, producing an enviable battlefield record in the war despite its relatively tiny size. Meanwhile, General John A. Lejeune proved Marine officers were just as professionally capable as their Army and Navy counterparts, rising to command the Army's 2d Division. The Marines earned the self-proclaimed title of "Devil Dogs" for heroic action at Belleau Wood, Soissons, Saint-Mihiel, Blanc Mont, and in the final Meuse-Argonne offensive (1918). Marine aviation also played a part in the war effort, flying day bomber missions over France and Belgium. The Marines' tenacity and ability to be media-savvy catapulted the Corps into even greater public conscientiousness, cementing their self-proclaimed reputation as an elite force into reality.

The 4th Marine Brigade was the first Marine unit to arrive in France. At first, the Marines were settled in a very quiet sector, but after 54 days of trench warfare they were ordered to protect Paris in the Aisne Defensive. In June 1918 the 4th Marine Brigade confronted the German Army at Belleau Wood.

The Germans initially made tremendous territorial gains but in their sector the Marines stalled the German offensive. They were ordered to counterattack and take Hill 142 to their direct front and the town of Bouresches. On June 6, a Marine battalion launched a fierce attack. After the hill was secured, three other Marine battalions attacked across a wheat field toward the town. Gunnery Sergeant Dan Daly led one of the charges across the

With "tin hats" and stripped for action down to light marching order packs, Leathernecks of the 55th Company, 5th Marines, form up in a village street for the march to the front. The Marines "came of age" during World War I, proving they were a world class fighting organization capable of taking on the best military forces in the world. (Still Picture Records Section [Record Group 128], NARA)

wheat fields, and is reported to have shouted, "Come on, you sons of bitches! Do you want to live forever?"

A three-war Marine, General Clifton Bledsoe Cates' career illustrates the Corps' transformation from a purely colonial infantry force into the large, professional Fleet Marine Force of the latter half of the 20th century; he became commandant of the Marine Corps in 1948. Interviewed in 1973 by Marine Corps' historians, he described one of his earliest engagements at Bouresches, France, during the battle of Belleau Wood:

> We were deployed across this wheat field and taking very heavy fire—my platoon was. We received word that Captain Duncan had been killed, the company commander. So with that I yelled to this Lieutenant Robertson, I said, "Come on, Robertson, let's go." And with that we jumped up and swarmed across that wheat field towards Bouresches. About two-thirds of the way I caught a machine gun round flush

Lieutenant Clifton B. Cates at Verdun in April, 1918. Many of the junior officers who fought during World War I went on to become senior officers during World War II. This continuity of service, combined with the action most saw in the Banana Wars in the 1920s and 1930s meant that the Marine Corps began World War II with a solid core of experienced officers and senior noncommissioned officers. (Collection of Clifton B. Cates/ COLL3157, Archives Branch, Marine Corps History Division)

on my helmet. It put a great big dent in my helmet and knocked me unconscious. So Robertson with the remainder of my platoon entered the west part of Bouresches. Evidently I must have been out for five or ten minutes. When I came to, I remember trying to put my helmet on and the doggone thing wouldn't go on. There was a great big dent in it as big as your fist.

The machine guns were hitting all around and it looked like hail. My first thought was to run to the rear. I hate to admit it, but that was it. Then I looked over to the right of the ravine and I saw four Marines in this ravine. So I went staggering over there—I fell two or three times, so they told me—and ran in and got these four Marines, and then about that time I saw Lieutenant Robertson who, with the remainder of my platoon, was leaving the western end of the town. By that time, we were right on the edge of the center of town. I yelled at him and I blew my whistle and he came over and he said, "All right, you take your platoon in and clean out the town and I'll get reinforcements" which I thought was a hell of a thing.

Well, anyway we did. We went on in and after getting into the town, we took heavy fire going down the streets. In fact, one clipped my helmet again and another hit me in the shoulder. We cleaned out most of the town, but by that time I had, I think it was, twenty-one men left.

Another legendary Marine at Belleau Wood was Sergeant Major John Quick, who received the Medal of Honor during the Spanish–American War for "signaling to the U.S.S. *Dolphin* on three different occasions while exposed to a heavy fire from the enemy." Twenty years later at Belleau Wood, Quick drove an ammo truck through intense enemy fire to re-supply Marines and received a Distinguished Service Cross.

On June 12, Marines broke the last German defensive line and the next day the Germans counterattacked, only to be repelled. The 4th Marine Brigade suffered massive casualties, more than the Corps had suffered over its entire history combined to that point. The French renamed Belleau Wood, "Bois de la Brigade de Marine" and awarded 4th Marine Brigade the "Croix de Guerre" for their actions in Belleau Wood.

The highest accolade came from their foes. Lieutenant Colonel Ernst Otto of the Historical Section of the German Army, writing about Marines fighting at Belleau Wood, said that "Their fiery advance and great tenacity were well recognized by their opponents."

Next came the battle of Soissons when 4th Marine Brigade became part of U.S. Army's 2d Infantry Division. Marshal Ferdinand Foch sent three divisions, including the 2d, directly into the German line near Soissons on July 18. During the battle, First Lieutenant Clifton B. Cates, commanding the 96th Company, sent back this iconic message: "I have only two out of my company and 20 out of some other company. We need support, but it is almost suicide to try to get it here as we are swept by machine gun fire and a constant barrage is on us. I have no one on my left and only a few on my right. I will hold." The attack was highly successful and the brigade was awarded a second "Croix de Guerre."

The Saint-Mihiel salient originally formed in the fall of 1914 during a wave of German offensives in the early stages of the war. The trenches along the salient saw drastic increases in fortification throughout the war. The 4th Marine Brigade at Saint-Mihiel was severely undermanned after numerous costly battles in the previous months. Fearing low numbers, troops from the U.S. Army were offered, but General John A. Lejeune felt it would damage the Marines' morale. Reinforcements for the Marines arrived on September 11, only one day before the attack began.

Artillery barrages began at 0100 on September 12 and troops started their attack later that day. The 2d Division entered the salient alongside the Army's I Corps. On September 13, General Lejeune ordered 4th Brigade to the frontlines and the Marines assumed the lead in the assault by 0400 on September 14. The next day was the hardest day of fighting for Marines, as the skies were controlled by German pilots, allowing Marines to be easily spotted for artillery marking. The German commander, General Max von Gallwitz, rushed reserves into the area, but by September 16, the salient had been pushed back dramatically.

The Marines' next test was the battle of Blanc Mont Ridge, after General John A. Lejeune took command of 2d Division. Blanc Mont was a test after General Lejeune refused to break the division up to reinforce French units and General Henri Gouraud, commander of the French 4th Army, agreed to keep the division intact if it took Blanc Mont. The Marines beat the German forces two hours after the attack began and the 4th Marine Brigade received its third "Croix de Guerre" for its actions at Blanc Mont, as well as the right to wear the *Fourragère*

During World War I the Marine Corps deployed two aviation units. The 1st Marine Aviation Force went to France in July 1918. These Marines flew with the U.S. Navy's Day Wing, Northern Bombing Group, attacking German U-boat bases along the Belgium coast. The 1st Aeronautic Company was sent to the Azores to hunt U-boats in the Atlantic in January 1918. The photograph shows a Marine seaplane in the Azores. Although they did not sink any U-boats, simply flying was dangerous enough as several Marines died during this deployment. (Official USMC photograph)

cords on their uniforms. Current members of the 5th and 6th Marines still wear the cords, but must doff them upon leaving the regiment.

The Meuse-Argonne Offensive was the final act for the Marines in the Great War. It was a major portion of the Hundred Days Offensive which ended the war. The battle began at 0530 on September 26 and lasted until November 11, the Armistice. During the offensive, Marines prepared to attack across Meuse River on November 10, 1918; news of the Armistice did not reach the Marines until they had forced a costly crossing of the river.

Besides fighting in France, Marines served in the Corps' first aerial units on anti-submarine patrols in the Atlantic and in a bombing campaign against Germany. Behind the lines the 5th Marine Brigade kept supplies moving to the front, and Marines served aboard U.S. Navy ships throughout the conflict. After the war, Marines served in the occupation army in Germany and at Vladivostok during America's intervention in the Russian civil war. The Corps emerged from World War I as an elite, modern fighting organization.

Lieutenant General John A. Lejeune was born January 10, 1867 on his family's plantation in Pointe Coupee Parish, Louisiana. He secured an appointment to the U.S. Naval Academy from which he graduated in 1888, then served two years as a midshipman at sea. He was serving aboard the sloop-of-war USS *Vandalia* (1876) in March 1889 when it was wrecked in a cyclone in Apia harbor during the Samoan crisis. He was commissioned into the Marine Corps as a second lieutenant in July 1890. He commanded the Marine detachment aboard the USS *Cincinnati* (C 7) during the Spanish–American War. He later twice commanded a Marine battalion in Panama.

In 1907, he commanded Marine Barracks and Naval Prison, Navy Yard, Cavite, Philippines, and took command of the 1st

Brigade of Marines in 1908. Following graduation from the U.S. Army War College in 1910, he again served in Cuba and Panama before becoming involved in the development of the advanced base regiment. He was promoted to brigadier general in 1916 and became assistant commandant of the Marine Corps.

Following America's entry into World War I, Lejeune deployed overseas, where he commanded the 4th Marine Brigade and the U.S. Army's 2d Infantry Division from July 1918 through August 1919. His performance commanding an Army division established that Marine Corps' officers were as professionally capable as their Army peers. He was awarded the Croix de Guerre and the Légion d'Honneur by the French government and both the U.S. Army and Navy's Distinguished Service Medals for his service during the war.

In July 1920 he was appointed Commandant of the Marine Corps; during his two terms, he reinvigorated Marine development of doctrine and strategic planning, and directed the Corps' transformation from a colonial infantry into an amphibious assault corps. In 1923, in a lecture to the Naval War College, he said, "[T]he major wartime mission of the Marine Corps is to support the Fleet by supplying it with a highly trained, fully equipped expeditionary force."

He retired from the Marine Corps in 1929 and became superintendent of the Virginia Military Institute, a position he held until 1937.

Throughout his career, General Lejeune remained determined to make the Marine Corps an elite fighting organization and a worthy expeditionary force for the U.S. Navy. When he passed away on November 20, 1942, Marines half a world away on Guadalcanal were proving just how successful he had been.

CHAPTER 4

————— ————— ————— —————

THE FLEET MARINE FORCE, 1920–1953

The performance of the Corps in the World War I had established its *bona fides* as a modern, professional, fighting organization. It was no longer in search of a mission; the officer corps had embraced the idea of Marines as the Navy's landing force, designed to seize and defend advanced naval bases. Marine zeal for this mission, which promised the Corps a specific role in the strategic calculus of America's defense, coincided with the growing realization with the rest of the American military that Japanese aggression in the Pacific was the most likely future threat to the interests of the United States.

Directed and supported by legendary Commandant Major General John A. Lejeune, Lieutenant Colonel Earl H. "Pete" Ellis produced the first doctrinal look at amphibious warfare and how it would fit into a Pacific campaign, but other Marines continued Ellis's work, notably future Commandant General Thomas Holcomb and General Holland M. Smith, "The Father of modern U.S. Amphibious Warfare." These Marines took the lessons in modern warfare that they had learned fighting a positional war of attrition in the mud of France, and applied them to land forces supporting a naval campaign in the Pacific. Reducing the Saint-Mihiel salient, for example, at first glance has little in common with securing a coral island such as Midway from powerful enemy land, sea, and air forces, but Marines recognized the underlying fundamentals of supply, training, and organization that modern warfare required for success in either field.

In *Coral and Brass* (1948), General Holland Smith said, "If the Battle of Waterloo was won on the playing fields of Eton, the Japanese bases in the Pacific were captured on the beaches of the Caribbean." The Corps did not merely create a doctrine for fighting its expected amphibious war in the Pacific; it experimented and trained for two decades. In the process the Corps developed specialized equipment and techniques for every aspect of amphibious assaults and amphibious landings.

At the same time, the Corps continued its traditional missions as colonial infantry, with service in Latin America and China. But even Marines traditionally associated with colonial warfare, such as Major General Smedley Butler, advanced their amphibious capabilities. Butler encouraged the development of the Christie amphibious tank for 1924 Fleet exercises, and commanded a combined-arms Marine brigade in China in the late 1920s, which was useful experience for Marines working with armor and aircraft while on expeditionary duty in a harsh environment. As the Marines' colonial infantry role slowly faded, the Corps produced the remarkable *Small Wars Manual* in 1940, capturing the lessons of such conflicts for later Marines.

When World War II finally arrived, the Marines Corps was ready, putting its plans for defending advanced naval bases to the test early at Wake Island and Midway. In August of 1942, the Corps put the entire concept to the test, seizing and then defending Guadalcanal from Japanese counterattacks. Throughout the rest of the war the Marines earned accolades as they refined and employed their amphibious warfare doctrine supporting the highly successful naval campaign which won the war against Japan.

Though the broad outlines of the war followed predictions first made by Ellis and other pre-war thinkers, technological changes altered the geographic realities of operations in the Pacific. The increased steaming ranges and the development of underway

Lieutenant General Thomas A. Holcomb, Commandant of the Marine Corps, Colonel Merritt A. Edson, and Major General Alexander A. Vandegrift during the lieutenant general's inspection on Guadalcanal, December 1942. Guadalcanal was the first counteroffensive launched by U.S. forces in World War II; holding the island was a difficult task but by December of 1942 it was accomplished. Soon after this the Marines would turn the island over to the Army who cleaned up the last of the Japanese resistance. (Official USMC photograph)

replenishment by the U.S. Navy reduced the need for advanced naval bases. But the dramatically increased value of airpower required airfields, and the Corps' techniques worked as well for seizing and defending islands for airfields as they did naval bases.

Marines were in the Pacific war from the start. On the morning of December 7, 1941, the Japanese planes that attacked the battle fleet riding at anchor in Pearl Harbor also attacked military airfields and other installations. Marines at the barracks fired on Japanese aircraft while Marines assigned to the battleships performed their duties aboard the doomed vessels. Within a few hours of the Pearl Harbor attack, Marines at Guam, Midway and Wake Island were also on the receiving end of Japanese bombs.

Captain Samuel R. Shaw, commander of a Marine Barracks company at Pearl Harbor, spoke with Marine Corps historians after the war about his experience on December 7, 1941:

The boat guards were in place, and the music was out there, and the old and new officer of the day. And we had a music, and a hell of a fine sergeant bugler who had been in Shanghai. He would stand beside the officers of the day, and there came the airplanes, and he looked up and he said, "Captain, those are Japanese war planes." And one of the two of them said, "My God, they are, sound the call to arms." So the bugler started sounding the call to arms before the first bomb hit.

Of course they had already started taking out the machine guns. They didn't wait for the key in the OD's office, they just broke the door down and hauled out the machine guns, put them in position. Everybody that wasn't involved in that drill grabbed their rifles and ran out in the parade ground, and started firing at the airplanes. They must have had several hundred men out there with rifles. And every [Japanese] plane that was recovered there, or pieces of it, had lots of .30-caliber holes—somebody was hitting them, machine guns or rifles.

Then I remembered—here we had all these guys on the post who had not been relieved, and they had been posted at 4 o'clock, and come 9 o'clock, 9:30 they not only had not been relieved but had no chow and no water. So I got hold of the mess sergeant and told him to organize, to go around to the posts.

They had a depot. At the beginning it was a supply depot. I told him to send a party over there and draw a lot of canteens and make sandwiches, and we'd send water and sandwiches around to the guys on posts until we found out some way to relieve all these guys, and get people back. Then he told me that it was fine except that he didn't have nearly enough messmen, they were all out in the parade ground shooting. I think the second phase of planes came in at that time and we had a hell of an uproar.

Guam was defended by only 153 Marines armed with nothing larger than .30 caliber machine guns. After two days of bombing, the defenders fought against the landing, but the odds against them were overwhelming and they were forced to surrender.

After three days of bombing, the Japanese moved in for a landing on Wake Island, defended by Major James P. S. Devereaux commanding a detachment of the 1st Defense Battalion and Major Paul A. Putnam's VMF-211. The Marines beat this first attack off, sinking two destroyers, damaging several more, and causing many enemy casualties. The Japanese responded with ten days of heavy bombing before returning with a larger landing force. The bombing campaign had finally worn down the squadrons fighting strength to nil and the pilots and ground crews now manned the lines as infantry. Despite a legendary defense, the island fell on December 21.

While Wake was being attacked, the Japanese were also invading the Philippines. Colonel Samuel L. Howard's 4th Marines, who had just arrived from Shanghai, were transferred to General MacArthur's command. The 4th Marines was now dramatically increased in size by the 1st Separate Marine Battalion, commanded by Lieutenant Colonel John P. Adams, previously based at the Cavite Navy Yard. These 700 Marines were organized both as a defense and an infantry battalion. MacArthur placed the Marines in charge of defending Corregidor and the tip of Bataan, where Marines manned antiaircraft batteries. These highly trained troops thus missed most of the Bataan fighting, but later fought fiercely against Japanese air attack and amphibious landings as the Japanese tried to outflank the Bataan defenders. Bataan fell on April 6, and Corregidor on May 6, 1942.

Marines poured into Midway prior to the Japanese attack on the island, with defenses organized around the 6th Defense Battalion and Marine Aircraft Group 22 (MAG-22). The attack came on June 4, 1942, but the U.S. Navy, aided by land-based air squadrons, won an overwhelming victory against the Japanese

Women Reservists first served in the Corps during World War I, but that experiment ended with the war. When World War II came around, the Corps was more resistant then the other services to accept women Marines, but they joined the Corps in 1943, serving in various jobs stateside in order to "Free a Marine to fight." Lieutenant General Thomas Holcomb, USMC, spoke in 1943:

> They [Women Marines] don't have a nickname, and they don't need one. They get their basic training in a Marine atmosphere, at a Marine Post. They inherit the traditions of the Marines. They are Marines.

fleet, sinking four carriers and driving off the Japanese landing force without any attempt at a landing.

In the early summer of 1942 the Japanese began construction of an airfield on Guadalcanal. They had also constructed a seaplane base 20 miles north on the island of Tulagi. These actions potentially signaled a revived Japanese advance in the South Pacific and threatened the flow of American aid to New Zealand and Australia. It was decided that lines of communication in South Pacific needed to be secured and Operation *Watchtower*—the seizure of Guadalcanal and Tulagi—was authorized.

Guadalcanal and Tulagi were Japanese forward outposts. The main Japanese naval and air forces in the South Pacific were located approximately 600 nautical miles away at Rabaul, New Britain. Headquartered there was the Eighth Fleet, Eleventh Air Fleet, and the 1st, 7th, 8th, and 14th Naval Base Forces. The Seventeenth Army was also assigned to the region, but was located at Rabaul. Intelligence on the number of Japanese defenders on Guadalcanal was poor. Seven to eight thousand defenders were expected but the actual number was 3,457 troops, and most of these were workers on the airfield there.

The airfield on Guadalcanal was the reason the island was so important. Japanese aircraft flying from the island could strike shipping traveling to Australia, so the Allies took the island. The airfield acted as an "unsinkable" aircraft carrier in the battles that followed, the Cactus Air Force, the Marine, Navy, and Army aircraft operated from the field, flying close-air support for the Marines on the ground and striking Japanese shipping, interdicting supplies that the Japanese starving on the island desperately needed. The photograph shows Grumman F4F Wildcat fighters parked on the fighter strip at Henderson Field. (Official USN photograph)

The 1st Marine Division was selected as the main landing force for Operation *Watchtower*. Major General Alexander A. Vandegrift commanded the 1st Marine Division. The division was comprised of three Marine Regiments, the 1st and 5th, and the 2d. The division was reinforced with the 1st Raider Battalion, 1st Parachute Battalion, and the 3d Defense Battalion.

Supporting the landing, Admiral Frank Jack Fletcher commanded three carriers, *Saratoga* (CV 3), *Enterprise* (CV 6), *Wasp* (CV 7), one battleship, *North Carolina* (BB 55), six cruisers and 16 destroyers. Fletcher was also in overall command of the expedition. In addition, Admiral Richard K. Turner commanded a covering force of five cruisers and nine destroyers. The plan was for the amphibious force to divide into two landing groups, landing group X-Ray, which would converge on the north shore of Guadalcanal, and landing group Yoke, which would head for Tulagi, Gavutu, Tanambogo, and Florida Island. These islands were 20 miles away from Guadalcanal across the Sealark Channel.

At 0909 on August 7, the first Marines landed on Guadalcanal. The first to land were the 5th Marines at Red Beach. The 1st Marines followed. The Marines met no resistance and immediately began to move inland towards the airfield. The Japanese troops, the majority of whom were Korean laborers, had fled and on August 8 the Marines captured the airfield and consolidated their positions.

The landings on the smaller islands across the channel were bitterly opposed. On Tulagi, the 1st Raider battalion, commanded by Lieutenant Colonel Edson, fought steadily through pockets of enemy resistance and by the end of the first night dug in overlooking the last enemy stronghold on the southern end of the island. The 2d Battalion, 5th Marines (2/5) also drove across the island and reached the north coast. During the night, the Japanese launched four separate attacks but lost the majority of their force. The island was captured by the afternoon of the 8th. Gavutu and Tanambogo were very small islands connected by a causeway. The Japanese endured the naval bombardment from within caves and were difficult to dislodge by the assaulting Marines on D-Day. After a rough night of close-in-fighting the remaining defenders were mopped up on the following day. In total 144 Marines were killed and 194 wounded. Few Japanese survived.

The Japanese responded quickly. On August 7, a flight of Japanese heavy bombers, light bombers, and fighters were intercepted by aircraft from Fletcher's carriers and the next night Japanese cruisers and destroyers launched a night attack on the blocking force ships Admiral Turner had placed at the western approaches to the Sealark Channel on the fleet. The battle of Savo Island was a rough American defeat, as four heavy cruisers were sunk and a fifth heavily damaged. The Japanese had only one cruiser damaged. The channel was given the name "Ironbottom Sound." The Navy also pulled back before delivering their full-supply loads of material, with one Marine regiment still aboard.

On August 12, the Marines completed the airfield's runway, utilizing captured Japanese equipment. The Marines established a perimeter around the airfield, and named it Henderson Field after a Marine bomber pilot who died in the battle of Midway. Also on August 12, a Marine patrol led by Lieutenant Colonel Frank Goettge, the division intelligence officer, was wiped out while attempting to receive "surrendering" Japanese troops. This incident increased the savagery of the war on Guadalcanal.

On August 20, the Marines were reinforced by 19 Grumman F4F-4 Wildcats of VMF-223 and 12 Douglas SBD-3 Dauntless dive bombers of VMSB-232. Later, five Army Bell P-400 Air Cobras arrived and nine more followed after. The island of Guadalcanal began to be known by its radio call sign "Cactus" and its air components were referred to as the "Cactus Air Force."

The Japanese believed the Marines only had about 2000 men on Guadalcanal. They sent a similar-sized force to the island under Colonel Kiyonao Ichiki, landing 25 miles from the Marine perimeter and struggling through the jungle towards the airfield. At 0130 on August 21, the Japanese troops charged the Marine lines along the Ilu River and were mowed down by Marines using machine guns and 37mm guns firing canister shells. The next morning Marine light tanks led a counter assault that completed the massacre.

Throughout September the Marines endured nightly bombing by aircraft and shelling by Japanese destroyers and cruisers while the Japanese worked to reinforce the island with another brigade of troops. Marine reinforcements arrived and on September 3, Brigadier General Roy Geiger, commander of 1st Marine Aircraft Wing, took over Cactus Air Force operations. Geiger's force protecting Guadalcanal in the air contained Marine, Navy, and Army aircraft.

Still underestimating Marine numbers on the island, General Kiyotake Kawaguchi's brigade made it to Guadalcanal, landing to the east of the Marine positions. Instead of attacking the heavily defended Marine perimeter on the east or west side of Henderson Field, Kawaguchi decided to move undetected through the jungle and over rough terrain to attack the thinly held Marine inland defensive line south of Henderson Field. The combined Marine parachute-raider battalion occupied Kawaguchi's avenue of approach, the prominent ridge south of Henderson Field. From September 12–15 the Japanese launched a series of night attacks against the Marine paras and raiders holding the ridge, and they were bloodily repulsed. The ridge was known from then on as either "Bloody Ridge" or "Edson's Ridge."

Major General Merritt Austin "Red Mike" Edson was born in 1897, he joined the Marine Corps Reserve on June 26, 1916, and was commissioned on October 9, 1917. He served with the 11th Marines in France and the occupation army of Germany. After the war he became a Marine Corps pilot, serving in the Pacific until physical reasons forced him to give up his flying status. He saw extensive action in Nicaragua in 1928–1929, and was awarded his first Navy Cross. He returned to the states for several training assignments, and in 1935 and 1936 he led the Marine Corps' national rifle and pistol teams as they won the national trophies both years. He served in Shanghai, China from 1937–1939, observing the Japanese military firsthand.

Edson took command of 1st Battalion, 5th Marines in June 1941. In January 1942 it began the process of being transformed into the 1st Raider Battalion. Edson led his battalion through the landings on Tulagi and the subsequent fighting on Guadalcanal. He told his men, "There it is. It is useless to ask ourselves why it is we who are here. We are here. There is only us between the airfield and the Japs. If we don't hold, we will lose Guadalcanal." He was awarded his second Navy Cross for the Tulagi assault. On the night of September 13–14, 1942 he led his battalion and the 1st Parachute Battalion in the defense of Lunga Ridge. The media called it "Bloody Ridge," but his men called it "Edson's Ridge," because he was "was all over the place, encouraging, cajoling, and correcting as he continually exposed himself to enemy fire." Edson was awarded the Medal of Honor by Roosevelt for his actions. Part of the citation reads:

> After the airfield on Guadalcanal had been seized from the enemy on August 8, Col. Edson, with a force of 800 men, was assigned to the occupation and defense of a ridge dominating the jungle on either side of the airport. Facing a formidable Japanese attack which, augmented by infiltration, had crashed through our front lines, he, by skillful handling of his troops, successfully withdrew his forward units to a reserve line with minimum casualties. When the enemy, in a subsequent series of violent assaults, engaged our force in desperate hand-to-hand combat with bayonets, rifles, pistols, grenades, and knives, Col. Edson, although continuously exposed to hostile fire throughout the night, personally directed defense of the reserve position against a fanatical foe of greatly superior numbers. By his astute leadership and gallant devotion to duty, he enabled his men, despite severe losses, to cling tenaciously to their position on the vital ridge, thereby retaining command not only of the Guadalcanal airfield, but also of the 1st Division's entire offensive installations in the surrounding area.

Following the conclusion of the Solomons campaign he served as Chief of Staff for the 2d Marine Division during the battle of Tarawa, for which he was awarded the Legion of Merit. He was promoted to Assistant Division Commander for the landings on Saipan and Tinian, for which he was awarded the Silver Star. He went on to serve as Chief of Staff and then Commanding General, Fleet Marine Force, Pacific.

Understanding now the size of the Marine garrison, the Japanese committed two divisions and significant naval forces to the recapture of Guadalcanal but the Americans also continued to reinforce. The 7th Marines arrive from Samoa; unfortunately the naval force that was protecting the convoys was mauled by Japanese submarines. The carrier *Wasp* (CV 7) and the destroyer *O'Brien* (DD 415) were sunk and the battleship *North Carolina* (BB 55) was damaged. Surviving aircraft from *Wasp* landed at Henderson and reinforced the Cactus Air Force.

General Vandegrift sought to expand his defensive position and decided to seize ground on the east bank of the Matanikau River. In early October the Marines fought a series of actions establishing a strong combat outpost on the east bank of the Matanikau, the most likely avenue of approach for the Japanese.

Even as the Marines fought hard against the Japanese, the jungle began to take its toll. Casualties from disease began to become a major issue and the number of men affected climbed to exceed battle casualties. These included crippling stomach cramps, "jungle rot" on the feet, and malaria. Malaria was so rampant that only Marines rendered completely prostrate by the disease were allowed to leave the line and rest in a field hospital. The Japanese supply lines were never as robust as the Marines, and they suffered even more from malnutrition and dehydration on the island, indeed, the Japanese renamed Guadalcanal, "Starvation Island."

On October 11, the U.S. Navy won the closely fought battle of Cape Esperance (Guadalcanal's western tip), bringing a sorely needed American naval victory and slowing the "Tokyo Express" of supplies and reinforcements to Guadalcanal.

On the night of October 13–14, Japanese 150mm howitzers opened up on the airfield along with the usual bombing and two Japanese battleships, *Kongo* and *Haruna*, moved into Ironbottom Sound to bombard the airfield and surrounding Marine positions. The airfield was hit hard but on the next day the aircraft that were still able to fly were sent out to attack Japanese aircraft and shipping.

The majority of the Sendai Division moved through the jungle to again attack the Marine perimeter from the south in the vicinity of Bloody Ridge, but Vandegrift knew of the upcoming attack. Marine forces were placed to protect the ridge as well as the east bank of the Matanikau River. On October 20–22, Japanese infantry accompanied by tanks tried to cross the Matanikau River and were repulsed by the strong Marine forces in the area and massed artillery fire.

Near midnight on October 24, the Japanese tried Bloody Ridge again, storming out of the jungle near the ridge with no supporting artillery or mortars. The Marines stopped them with artillery, mortar, and interlocking machinegun fire, then, after a series of counterattacks, were able to straighten their lines. The recently arrived 164th Infantry reinforced Lieutenant Colonel Puller's Marine line, and attacks on the Marine and Army troops continued through the night. On the night of October 25, the Japanese attacked the same as before, with similar results. The Sendai Division offensive was over.

During the October 24–25 battles two Marines acted "above and beyond the call of duty" and were awarded the Medal of Honor, Sergeant John Basilone of 1st Battalion, 7th Marines and Platoon Sergeant Mitchell Paige of 2d Battalion, 7th Marines. In total, ten Marines would be bestowed the Medal of Honor from actions occurring during the Guadalcanal Campaign. Five Marine flyers of the Cactus Air Force would earn the distinction: Captain Harold W. Bauer; Captain Jefferson J. DeBlanc (VMF-112), Captain Joseph J. Foss (VMF-121); Major Robert E. Galer (VMF-224); and Major John L. Smith (VMF-223). Colonel Edson would receive the Medal of Honor for his actions in defense of "Edson's Ridge," and Major General Vandegrift, for his role through the entire campaign. Corporal Anthony Casamento, a machinegun squad leader from 1st Battalion, 5th Marines, had his Navy Cross upgraded to a Medal of Honor in 1980.

The Navy fought the bloody battle of Santa Cruz, a draw in which the USS *Hornet* was sunk. The American flyers came out a little ahead, however, as they lost 74 planes to the 100 lost by the Japanese.

Receiving further reinforcements, in November General Vandegrift forestalled further Japanese offensives by clearing the area immediately west of the Matanikau. The Marines faced fierce enemy resistance near the shore area but pushed through to Point Cruz. On November 3, the pocket of Japanese defenders just west of Point Cruz was destroyed, killing over 300 enemy soldiers.

Meanwhile, the 2d Marine Raider Battalion, commanded by Lieutenant Colonel Evans F. Carlson, landed at Aola Bay (40 miles to the east of the Marine perimeter) and swept west on the "Long Patrol." They aggressively pursued the Japanese retreating through the jungle, clearing the area east of Henderson of significant Japanese forces.

The Navy fought two fierce night actions off Guadalcanal from November 12–15, forcing the Japanese to retire on the first night, and on the second night the battleships *Washington* (BB 56) and *South Dakota* (BB 55), with a four destroyer escort, intercepted the Japanese and won a costly victory. Both American battleships were badly damaged but the Japanese lost the *Kirishima* entirely. The transports the Japanese fleet was escorting were run aground or sunk, and pounded by aircraft from Henderson Field throughout the day. Large-scale Japanese reinforcement of Guadalcanal was over.

With the threat to Guadalcanal eased, the 1st Marine Division was replaced by the Army's 25th Infantry Division and on December 9 an Army commander, General Alexander M. Patch, replaced General Vandergrift as commander of operations in Guadalcanal. On December 7, 1942, the one-year anniversary of Pearl Harbor, Vandergrift told the men on Guadalcanal that their "unbelievable achievements had made Guadalcanal a synonym for death and disaster in the language of our enemy." Guadalcanal was the first American offensive of World War II and from then onward the United States would remain on the offensive in the Pacific.

But fighting in the Solomons was not over. In order to protect the flank of U.S. Army and Australian troops fighting in New

Following the successful Guadalcanal campaign, the Allies moved "up the slot" of the Solomon island chain. This required the Marines to make many small amphibious landings like this one, where Marines waded ashore on D-Day at Bougainville, as seen from a beached LCVP. Bougainville was the northern most island of the chain, and the campaign to take it was the culmination of the operations to seize the Solomons. (Official USMC photograph)

Guinea, Marine and Army troops began a series of amphibian "hops" up the Solomon island chain throughout 1943, driving "up the Slot" until they reached Bougainville, at the northwest end. In this campaign Marine aircraft supplied the close-air support, carrying out bombing and strafing missions as close as 75 yards from the Marines' front line.

In November 1943, the Navy and Marines began the long-planned drive across the central Pacific, intended to ring the Japanese Navy to battle and allow the Navy to blockade Japan and force an end to the war. This was the basics of War Plan Orange, developed before the war in case of war with Japan. The Marine's job was to seize the advanced naval bases required to follow the

During the Solomons campaign the Marines began to use **war dogs** to provide support in jungle warfare. One of the first Marine commanders to use them on patrol, Captain Wilcie O'Bannon, later described their use, "One dog was a German Shepherd female, the other was a Doberman male, and they had three men with them. The third man handled the dogs all the time in the platoon area prior to our going on patrol—petting the dogs, talking to them, and being nice to them. The other two handlers—one would go to the head of the column and one would go to the rear with the female messenger dog.... If the dog in front received enemy fire and got away, he could either come back to me or circle to the back of the column. If I needed to send a message I would write it, give it to the handler, and he would pin it on the dog's collar. He would clap his hands and say, 'Report,' and the dog would be off like a gunshot to go to the third man in the rear who had handled him before the patrol."

strategy, proving that they could seize heavily defended islands despite well-known failures like the Allied landings at Gallipoli during World War I.

The first island stronghold which needed to be taken was Tarawa in the Gilbert Islands. Major General Holland M. Smith, commanding the V Amphibious Corps, assigned this task to the 2d Marine Division. Tarawa was bombed and shelled for three days. The 2d Division landed on November 20, 1943, crawling across the reef that surrounded Tarawa in amtracs, the first use of amtracs as combat vehicles. The Japanese defended the beach with murderous fire, inflicting heavy casualties. Colonel David M. Shoup commanded the initial landing forces on Tarawa and was wounded on the first day, for which he was awarded the Medal of Honor. He reported from the beach, "Casualties many; Percentage of dead not known; Combat efficiency; we are winning."

General Holland "Howlin' Mad" Smith was the father of modern amphibious warfare, one of the marines who worked tirelessly to develop amphibious doctrine between the wars and then the Marine commander most committed to carrying that doctrine out in the Pacific where he command the V Amphibious Corps, conducting the amphibious assaults in the central pacific drive.

Smith was known for his fierce temper and antagonism to the Army. But his more human side was on display when he toured Tarawa following the bloody battle. Accompanied by fellow officers and the journalist Robert Sherrod, "Howlin' Mad" came upon a dead Marine, leaning forward against the seawall, "one arm still supported upright by the weight of his body. On top of the seawall, just beyond his upraised hand, lies a blue and white flag, a beach marker to tell succeeding waves where to land." General Smith cleared his throat and said, "How can men like that ever be defeated?"

It took three days of vicious fighting, but the Marines took the island. They also suffered over 3,300 casualties while less than 200 of the 4,800 defenders survived. The casualties caused an uproar in the United States, but the Corps had proven the soundness of its amphibious warfare doctrine.

War Plan Orange had called for a thrust through the central pacific at Japan, but American politics and the vicissitudes of the war placed the first Allied offensive in the south-west Pacific, in the Solomon island chain. General MacArthur, commanding in the south-west Pacific, pushed to abandon the central pacific drive and instead support his own drive to return to the Philippines, which he had vowed to liberate after he was defeated there by the Japanese army. Rather than choose, Allied strategists in 1943 decided to shift between the central Pacific drive and MacArthur's drive through the south-west towards the Philippines.

In the south-west Pacific, the 3d Marine Division was fighting in the Solomons, while the 1st Marine Division seized the western end of New Britain. Then the 1st Marine Division landed at Cape Gloucester, New Britain, on the opposite end of the island from Rabaul. After four months of combat for the Marines to secure one third of New Britain, the remainder of New Britain was bypassed and the Marines turned the island over to Army units on April 25, 1944.

After the Gilbert Islands, Major General Smith's V Amphibious Corps turned its attention to the Marshals. In early

The Marine Corps proved that it could take heavily fortified and well-defended islands away from determined defenders, something that was considered nigh-impossible after the Allies' World War I disaster at Gallipoli. As supporting naval and air units paved the way with high explosives, Marine-laden assault craft formed the first wave and moved in for the attack on Peleliu in the Palau Islands. The Leathernecks hacked out a mile-and-a-half-long beachhead, and after bitter fighting, began the advance on the Japanese airfield. (Official USMC photograph)

1944 Kwajalein, Roi-Namur, and Eniwetok were taken. These conquests enabled the capture of other islands in the Marshal Group while islands not essential for bases were bypassed and assigned to Marine air units for neutralization.

Next came the Marianas, where the V and III Amphibious Corps, comprised of Army and Marine divisions, attacked, starting in June, 1944. First was Saipan, only nine days after the Allies landed in Normandy in the European war, followed by the liberation of Guam in July, a much larger island that required a longer campaign to secure. Simultaneously Tinian was taken in just nine days. After three solid weeks of almost continuous fighting, Guam was announced as secured on August 10, 1944, completing the conquest of the Marianas.

That fall Marines fought on Peleliu as the south and central Pacific offensives converged, with Marine air supporting the Army's campaign to liberate the Philippines.

After the Philippine campaign was underway there remained the islands that the Allies intended to take before considering an invasion of Japan—Iwo Jima and Okinawa. The first of these was

Marines have always left a strong impression on the **war correspondents** who served with them. This began in 1898 when Stephen Crane's reporting from Guantanamo Bay first made the Corps famous and continued in World War II. Journalist Ernie Pyle, who won the Pulitzer for his everyman accounts of American soldiers, had this to say about Marines: "Marines have a cynical approach to war. They believe in three things; liberty, payday and that when two Marines are together in a fight, one is being wasted. Being a minority group militarily, they are proud and sensitive in their dealings with other military organizations. A Marine's concept of a perfect battle is to have other Marines on the right and left flanks, Marine aircraft overhead and Marine artillery and naval gunfire backing them up."

Iwo Jima. The V Amphibious Corps, comprising the 3d, 4th, and 5th Marine Divisions was ordered to take Iwo Jima. They landed on February 19, 1944 and fought one of the toughest battles to date in the Pacific War against fanatical Japanese defenders who dug in deeply and fought a fierce delaying action designed to inflict maximum casualties on the Americans—the Japanese defenders fought nearly to the last man. On February 23, a patrol from the 28th Marines was ordered to raise a flag over Mount Suribachi. The first flag raised was considered too small, so a second flag was sent up the mountain and raised. Associated Press photographer Joe Rosenthal took the legendary picture of this second flag raising which has since become an enduring symbol of victory and the image chosen for the famous Marine Corps Memorial in Washington, D.C. But despite the flag raising, many days of fighting remained before Iwo Jima was secured. Observing the flag raising from a naval vessel, James Forrestal, Secretary of the Navy, said "The raising of that flag on Suribachi means a Marine Corps for the next 500 years."

On March 16, 1945, the island was officially declared secure, but the Japanese continued to appear from tunnels and harass the Americans. On March 25, 300 Japanese soldiers launched a surprise night attack on one of the airfields that inflicted over 150 casualties before the Japanese were all killed. The last Japanese defenders of Iwo Jima didn't surrender until 1949. Admiral Chester W. Nimitz later praised those who attacked the island, saying "Among the Americans who served on Iwo Island uncommon valor was a common virtue."

Okinawa was the last amphibious campaign of World War II, seized as a staging ground for a possible invasion of Japan proper. It was a massive operation, fought by the Tenth Army, commanded by Lieutenant General Simon B. Buckner, Jr. USA. The assault forces consisted of the Army's XXIV Corps (4 infantry divisions) and the III Amphibious Corps, composed of the 1st and 6th Marine Divisions. The 2d Marine Division was kept afloat in reserve.

The flag raising on Iwo Jima was a prosaic moment in the Pacific campaign, a mundane Marine patrol ascending a mountain and planting two flags in succession, as ordered. But Joe Rosenthal's iconic image of the second flag raising became an enduring symbol of victory following a long, bloody campaign, and served as the inspiration for an impressive monument to Marines past and present in Washington D.C. ("Flag Raising, Mt. Suribachi Iwo Jima" painted by Sergeant Tom Lovell. Art Collection, National Museum of the Marine Corps)

Early on the morning of April 1, 1945, leading waves of the assault troops landed on Okinawa but there was no curtain of deadly fire. The Japanese had concentrated the majority of their force at the rugged southern end of the island, leaving delaying forces in the north, in order to slow the American conquest and inflict the maximum number of casualties possible on the U.S. forces. The Japanese launched the first massive waves of kamikaze attacks against the allied naval forces. They failed to sink any carriers but they sank smaller vessels and damaged several carriers.

On Okinawa proper the Japanese fought tenaciously, with the civilian population forced to aid in the defense. Dug in securely in well-planned positions, Okinawa was a glimpse of how ferocious fighting on Japan proper would have been. On June 18, General Buckner was killed by enemy fire while watching a Marine unit assault an objective. Marine Major General Roy Geiger assumed command of the Tenth Army, becoming the first Marine officer to command an Army unit of this size. On June 21, the last pockets of Japanese resistance were eliminated, and Okinawa was secured.

During the two decades before World War II, the Marine Corps began to develop in earnest the doctrine, equipment, and organization need for amphibious warfare. The success of this effort was proven first on Guadalcanal, then on Bougainville, Tarawa, New Britain, Kwajalein, Eniwetok, Saipan, Guam, Tinian, Peleliu, Iwo Jima, and Okinawa. By the end of the war in 1945, the Marine Corps had grown to include six divisions, five air wings, and supporting troops. Its strength in World War II peaked at 485,113.

When World War II ended, the military found itself facing massive budget cuts as the nation returned to peacetime norms. In the wake of the nuclear bombs dropped on Hiroshima and Nagasaki, a lot of change and unrest was in the air for the U.S. defense establishment. The Army Air Corps successfully lobbied to become a new service, and some in the Army attempted to have the Marine Corps subsumed into the army, disbanded, or reduced to a token force.

The Corps struggled hard to preserve its existence, an ironic struggle considering that the Pacific war had proven it could perform the function it claimed for itself— acting as an expeditionary strike force. Testifying before the Senate Naval Affairs Committee, Commandant of the Marine Corps General Alexander A. Vandergrift gave an eloquent speech: "The Marine Corps … believes that it has earned this right—to have its future decided by the legislative body which created it—nothing more. Sentiment is not a valid consideration in determining questions of national security. We have pride in ourselves and in our past, but we do not rest our case on any presumed ground of gratitude owing us from the Nation. The bended knee is not a tradition of our Corps. If the Marine as a fighting man has not made a case for himself after 170 years of service, he must go. But I think you will agree with me that he has earned the right to depart with dignity and honor, not by subjugation to the status of uselessness and servility planned for him by the War Department."

In 1947 the organization of the Army was altered, a new department of the Air Force was created, and along with the Department of the Army and the Department of the Navy, was placed beneath the new Department of Defense. The Corps' hard lobbying paid off as the National Security Act of 1947 spelled out the roles and missions of the various services, specifying that the Marine Corps should include land combat and service forces plus organic aviation units. Further, "The Marine Corps shall be organized to provide fleet marine forces of combined arms, together with supporting air components, for service with the fleet in the seizure or defense of advanced naval bases," and Marines were to be responsible for development of amphibious techniques, provide for the protection of naval bases, and perform other services at the direction of the president.

Despite the legislative victories, the Corps still had powerful enemies. When Congressman Gordon L. McDonough suggested that the Marine Corps be entitled to full recognition as a major branch of the armed forces, President Harry S. Truman replied "The Marine Corps is the Navy's police force and as long as I am president that is what it will remain. They have a propaganda machine that is almost equal to Stalin's." With Marines fighting in Korea when he said this, President Truman was forced to apologize but the Corps' junior status in the Department of Defense remained. The dramatic opening of the Atomic Age had put the Corps' future in doubt, especially for those who believed its usefulness was limited to dramatic amphibious assaults against heavily fortified beaches. While Marine units were taking part in the occupation of Japan (1945–46) and North China (1945–49), studies were being undertaken at Quantico, Virginia, which concentrated on attaining a "vertical envelopment" capability for the Corps through the use of helicopters.

The Korean War put the Corps' concepts to the test again. A Marine brigade was in Korea by August 1950, supported by a Marine air group and illustrating the power and flexibility of the Marine air-ground team. Landing at Inchon, Korea, Marines proved that the doctrine of amphibious assault was still viable and necessary. After the recapture of Seoul, the Marines advanced to the Chosin Reservoir only to see the Chinese Communists enter the war. After years of offensives, counteroffensives, seemingly endless trench warfare, and occupation duty, the last Marine ground troops were withdrawn in March 1955.

On June 25, 1950, the Russian-trained North Korean People's Army (NKPA) attacked the Republic of Korea (ROK). Within a month South Korean and U.S. troops were holding a small beachhead around the southeastern seaport of Pusan. There were few if any Marines in Korea when the war broke out, but by mid-July the 1st Provisional Marine Brigade sailed for Korea.

On arrival in Pusan the brigade was ordered to "plugging holes in the dike," reinforcing the defensive lines as weak spots opened up, acting as the perimeter's "fire brigade." MAG-33 had arrived in Japan with Corsairs and was flying close-air support missions from the decks of escorts carriers off the coast. On three separate occasions the brigade, supported by Marine air, counterattacked the enemy and stopped his attack, eliminating the penetration.

The 1st Marine Division, commanded by Major General Oliver P. Smith, absorbed the brigade, and arrived off the coast of Korea by September 14. The lst Marine Aircraft Wing arrived to provide air support. General MacArthur wanted to land at Inchon with the 1st Marine Division in order to cut off and destroy North Korean forces as the rest of the South Korean and allied forces attacked north from the Pusan perimeter.

Five days of continual pounding by air and naval gunfire preceded the arrival of the assault troops at Inchon on the morning of September 15. The first landing was on Wolmi-do, an island that dominated the approaches to Inchon and was held by the North Koreans. Marines had to seize it in the early hours before the landings at Inchon in order to neutralize any artillery present.

Lieutenant Colonel Robert D. Taplett's 3d Battalion, 5th Marines was assigned the duty of taking the island, which was first strafed by Marine Corsairs and then hammered by naval guns and rockets prior to the 0633 September 15, 1950 landing of the first wave of assault troops. The Marines faced only light resistance in this early morning assault, the second wave landing hard on the heels of the first, and third wave of 10 tanks landing at 0646. H and G companies continued to sweep across the island towards their objectives. First Lieutenant Robert D. Bohn's G Company "was to land to the right of Green Beach in the assault, wheel right, and seize the dominant hill mass on the island, Radio Hill." Resistance continued to be light as Bohn's company climbed the 105 meter high hill. The top of the hill was reached and at 0655 3d Platoon guide Sergeant Alvin E. Smith tied the flag to tree at the top of a tree. General Douglas McArthur was observing the landing from the USS *Mount McKinley* (AGC 7) and upon observing the flag he said, "That's it. Let's get a cup of coffee."

By 0800 the Marines had occupied all of the main island, and cleared out a couple nests of North Korean soldiers although resistance remained light. Lieutenant Colonel Taplett radioed that the island was secure, and General MacArthur took the opportunity to send a hyperbolic message to Vice Admiral Arthur D. Struble, commander of the invasion fleet, "The Navy and Marines have never shone more brightly than this morning." Fighting was not over, however, as Marines and tanks advanced along a causeway to the So Wolmi-do islet at 1000 and after a short but fierce firefight secured that part of the island as well.

That evening the 5th Marines and 1st Marines began their landings at Inchon, climbing the seawall against fierce opposition and assaulting the city. After taking an important objective covering the landing beaches, Observatory Hill, by assault that evening, the 5th Marines staged another dramatic flag raising on the radio tower at its crest.

During the battle of Seoul, just days later, Colonel Lewis B. "Chesty" Puller, then commander of the 1st Marines, passed on an American flag and ordered that the first of his units to seize an objective within the Seoul city limits raise the flag, clearly intending this to echo the iconic Iwo image. When the 1st Marines seized Hill 79 after a tense river crossing in DUKWs and a rapid assault on the hill's defenders, Captain Robert H. Barrow's Company A, 1st Battalion, 1st Marines, which had taken point on the assault, was given the honor of raising this flag. Legendary *Life* magazine photographer and Marine veteran David Douglas Duncan captured the image for posterity. There were criticisms of this flag raising, as Captain Barrow later said, "Putting the flag on a bamboo pole over a peasant's house on the edge of Seoul does not constitute retaking the city."

Seoul proved to be difficult to liberate, despite the desires of General Douglas MacArthur and General Edward M. Almond to quickly declare the mission accomplished. Veteran North Korean forces defended Seoul and the 1st Marine Division was forced into bloody street fighting in order to subdue them. On September 25 the battle for Seoul began in earnest, the following days of heavy fighting reduced much of the city to ruins, as North Koreans had to be forced from position after position by artillery, air strikes, assault and flamethrowers.

On September 27 the regiments began a friendly competition to raise flags over Seoul as North Korean resistance began to crumble. The 5th Marines tore down the North Korean flags over the Seoul government compound and raised an American flag there instead. Not to be outdone, the 1st Marines looked to consulates as their flag targets. The race was described in *U.S. Marines in the Korean War* (History Division, 2007):

> As the lead battalions of both regiments lengthened their strides, a sense of friendly rivalry spurred them into a race to raise the national colors over key landmarks. The 1st Marines fought their way into several embassies, led by Company E, pausing to raise the flag over first the French, then the Soviet (with great irony), and finally the United States residences. Growled one gunnery sergeant: "It looks like the 4th of July around here."

These incidents led to one of the many apocryphal tales which clung to the legendary "Chesty" Puller, recounted in Burke Davis's *Marine! The Life of Chesty Puller*: "An officer from Almond's headquarters growled, 'Ever since that flag-raising on Iwo Jima, I'm convinced that a Marine had rather carry a flag than a weapon.' 'Not a bad idea,' Puller replied, 'A man with a flag in his pack and a desire to put it on an enemy strongpoint isn't likely to bug out.'"

Following the Inchon assault and the liberation of Seoul, the 1st Marine Division moved north with the rest of the allied forces, driving the North Koreans towards the Chinese border. The division found itself in the Chosin Reservoir region as winter was setting in November 1950 when the Chinese came across the border *en masse*, determined to sweep away the South Korean and allied forces. The 1st Marine Division found itself nearly cut off and assaulted by multiple Chinese divisions. On December 1, Major General Oliver P. Smith, commander of the 1st Marine Division, ordered his troops to fight their way south as a division. Completely surrounded by Communist armies, press correspondents asked the commanding general if he intended to retreat. Smith replied, "Retreat hell! We're just attacking in another direction." Colonel "Chesty" Puller was just as blunt rallying his men, "Don't you forget that you're Marines—First Marines! Not all the communists in hell can overrun you!"

The conditions were icy, they were outnumbered and surrounded, but the Marines enjoyed excellent close-air support from the Marine squadrons flying above them, and they fought the Chinese divisions to a standstill while they continually moved south towards the harbor at Hungnam. There they boarded ship and moved back into South Korea.

The 1st Marine Division's withdrawal from the Chosin Reservoir in 1950, fighting against 10 Chinese infantry divisions, is perhaps the most legendary of all of the Marine Corps' battles. Here, troops of Regimental Combat Team 7 wait just south of Hagaru-ri while Marine and naval close-air support work over enemy positions with napalm on December 6, 1950. (Oliver P. Smith Collection (COLL/213), Archives Branch, Marine Corps History Division)

When the 1st Marine Division had fought its way out and was shipped south, Major General Smith wrote a letter to the Commandant of the Marine Corps describing the division's actions during the Chosin campaign. This clearly written letter dated December 19, 1950, remains an excellent summary of the campaign from the Marine point of view:

At the present moment I am in Masan. I sailed on the U.S.S. *Bayfield* from Hungnam on December 15th for Pusan. With the exception of certain Shore Party elements, elements of the AmphTrac Battalion, and NGF teams and TAC Parties, which are being retained by Corps at Hungnam for the time being, the entire division should close Masan today. What our mission will be I do not know. When the remainder of the X Corps arrives in the Pusan area, the Corps will become a part of the 8th Army. Lem Shepherd has made representations to Corps regarding the need for a period of time in which the division can integrate replacements, repair equipment, and be resupplied. The Corps is aware of this need, not only for us but also for the 7th Division, which lost practically en toto two infantry battalions and a field artillery battalion. However, Corps will not be calling the turns here.

You have probably read a lot of misinformation in the newspapers and it might be well to give you a factual account of what we have been doing for the past two weeks.

When I last wrote you the 8th Army had not yet launched its attack. At that time my mission was to establish a blocking position at Yudam-ni and with the remainder of the division to push north to the Manchurian border. As I explained to you, I did not press the 5th and 7th Marines, which had reached the Chosin Reservoir, to make any rapid advances. I wanted to proceed cautiously for two reasons. First, I had back of me fifty miles of MSR, fourteen miles of which was a tortuous mountain road which could be blocked by bad weather, and I wanted to accumulate at Hagaru-ri at the southern end of the reservoir a few days supply of ammunition and rations before proceeding further. Secondly, I wanted to move Puller up behind me to protect the MSR and he had not yet been entirely released from other commitments.

By November 23d both the 5th and 7th Marines were in contact with the CCF, the 5th to the east of the Chosin Reservoir and the 7th to the west thereof. The 7th was advancing to the blocking position assigned by Corps at Yudam-ni. In the fifteen-mile stretch of road between Hagaru-ri and Yudam-ni the 7th had to traverse a 4000 foot mountain pass and was impeded by the enemy, road blocks, and snow drifts. Patrols of the 5th pushed to the north end of the reservoir.

On November 24th the 8th Army 9s attack jumped off. With the attack came General MacArthur 1s communique which explained the "massive compression envelopment" that was to take place. I learned for the first time that the 1st Marine Division was to be the northern "pincers" of this envelopment. At a briefing on November 25th the details were explained. I was to make the main effort of the Corps in a zone of action oriented to the westward. I was to advance along the load from Yudam-ni toward Mupyong-ni, cut the road and railroad there, send one column on to the Manchurian border at Kuup-tong, and another column north to Kanggyeo The 7th Infantry Division was to take over my former mission of advancing north up the east side of the reservoir and thence to the Manchurian border. The 3d Infantry Division was to take over the protection of the MSR up to Hagaru-ri. (This never transpired and to the end of the operation I had to retain one battalion of the 1st Marines at Chinhung-ni at the foot of the mountain and another battalion of the 1st Marines at Koto-ri at the top of the mountain. otherwise there would have been no protection for this vital part of the MSR). Under the plan the Corps assumed responsibility for engineer maintenance of the MSR to Hagaru-ri. It also agreed to stock ten days supplies at Hagaru-ri. I doubt if the corps would have been able to do this. In any event the enemy gave us no opportunity to prove whether or not it could be done.

D-Day, H-Hour for the attack to the westward was fixed by Corps as 27 November, 0800. By November 26th Litzenberg, with all of the 7th, was at Yudam-ni. I decided to have him remain in the Yudam-ni area and pass the 5th through him for the attack to the westward. The 5th had not been in a serious engagement since the attack on Seoul.

The attack jumped off on schedule but it was not long before both the 5th and 7th were hit in strength by the CCF. By November 28th reports of casual ties left no doubt as to the seriousness of the attack. At the same time the 8th Army front was crumbling. No word was received from Corps regarding discontinuance of the attack or withdrawal. Under the circumstances I felt it was rash to have Murray attempt to push on and I directed him to consolidate on the positions he then held west of Yudam-ni. At the same time I directed Litzenberg to open up the MSR between Yudam-ni and Hagaru-ri which had been blocked by the Chinese, as had also the stretch of road between Hagaru-ri and Koto-ri. On this same day, November 28th, I moved my operational CP to Hagaru-ri. The movement was made by helicopter, the only feasible method in view of the cutting of the MSR. Fortunately, we had been able to get some vehicles and working personnel into Hagaru-ri before the road was cut.

Litzenberg's efforts to clear the MSR between Yudam-ni and Hagaru-ri were unsuccessful on the 28th. He reported he would make another effort with a battalion the following day, November 29th.

On November 28th Puller organized Task Force Drysdale to open up the MSR between Koto-ri and Hagaru-ri. This force was under command of LtCol Drysdale of the RM Commandos. It consisted of the RM Commandos, 235 strong, G Company of 3/1 coming north to join its parent unit at Hagaru-ri, and a rifle company of the 31st Infantry which was moving north to join its parent unit east of the

Chosin Reservoiro (The 7th Infantry Division had pushed north a battalion of the 31st, a battalion of the 32d, and a field artillery battalion to relieve the 5th Marines on the east side of the Chosin Reservoir.) In addition to the units enumerated, the Drysdale column included two companies of our M-26 tanks, each less a platoon, and a truck convoy. The column was to move out on the 29th. I will cover its operations later.

During the night of November 28–29 the enemy attacked Hagaru-ri in force. The attack started at 2130 and lasted all night. First the attack came in from the south, then shifted to the west and then to the east. Our defense force consisted of 3/1, less G Company, and personnel of our Headquarters and Service units. Our casualties were 500, of whom about 300 were from the infantry and 200 from Headquarters and Service units. The Headquarters Battalion alone had 60 casualties.

We had at an early date realized the importance of Hagaru-ri as a base. On November 16th Field Harris and I had tentatively approved a site for a C-47 strip at Hagaru-ri. Work was begun by our 1st Engineer Battalion on November 19th and the strip was first used by C-47s on December 1st, although at the time it was only 40% completed. This strip was essential for the evacuation of wounded and air supply in case our road went out either due to weather or enemy action. Hagaru-ri had to be held to protect this strip and the supplies which we were accumulating there. The movement of the Drysdale column from Koto-ri to Hagaru-ri would not only open the road, but would also furnish us needed reinforcements for the defense of Hagaru-ri.

The Drysdale column started north from Koto-ri on the morning of November 29th. About halfway to Hagaru-ri it became engaged in a heavy fire fight. Embarrassed as he was by a truck convoy, Drysdale was on the point of turning back to Koto-ri, but I sent him a message to push on through if at all possible. He started the truck convoy back toward

Koto-ri under the protection of a company of tanks and some infantry while the remainder of the column continued to fight its way toward Hagaru-ri. The truck convoy returning to Koto-ri was jumped by the Chinese who had closed in on the MSR again. There was considerable mortar fire and tanks as well as trucks were pretty badly shot up before they got back to Koto-ri. There were also a considerable number of personnel casualties. Drysdale continued to fight on toward Hagaru-ri and toward evening arrived with about 150 of his Commandos and G Company of the 1st Marines. The Army Company never arrived although some stragglers came in to Koto-ri. The conclusion was inescapable that a considerable force would be required to open up the MSR between Hagaru-ri and Koto-ri. We would not have any such force until the 5th and 7th Marines joined us at Hagaru-ri.

On November 29th the 7th Marines started a battalion back along the MSR to open up it, but the battalion got nowhere. I then ordered Litzenberg to employ the entire 7th Marines on the following day, November 30th, to open up the MSR. At the same time I ordered Murray to pull back his regiment to Yudam-nio Late in the day of November 29th I received a telephone call (radio link) from Corps stating that the whole scheme of maneuver was changed, that the Army battalions on the east side of the Chosin Reservoir, who were now cut off from us were attached to me and I was to extricate them, and that I was to withdraw the 5th and 7th Marines and consolidate around Hagaru-ri.

On November 30th the Corps turned over to me command of all troops as far south as Sudong, which is four or five miles below the foot of the mountain. These comprised a battalion of the 31st Infantry which was on its way up the mountain and miscellaneous engineer and service units.

During the day of November 30th Puller was attacked rather heavily at Koto-ri but kept his perimeter intact.

On the afternoon of November 30th General Almond flew up to see me. By this time he had given up any idea of consolidating positions in the vicinity of Hagaru-ri. He wanted us to fall back in the direction of Hamhung and stressed the necessity for speed. He authorized me to burn or destroy equipment and supplies, stating that I would be supplied by air drop as I withdrew. I told him that my movements would be governed by my ability to evacuate the wounded, that I would have to fight my way back and could not afford to discard equipment, and that, therefore, I intended to bring out the bulk of my equipment.

The problems of the 5th and 7th Marines could not be separated. By November 30th, between them, they had accumulated about 450 wounded who had to be protected. The only feasible thing to do was to pool their resources. The two regimental commanders drew up a joint plan (an ADC would have come in handy at this point) which was flown to me by helicopter and which I approved. Briefly, the 7th was to lead out from Yudam-ni and the 5th was to cover the rear. Artillery and trains were in the middle. The walking wounded were given weapons and marched in column on the road. Other wounded were loaded in trucks. The route these two regiments had to traverse was tortuous. From Yudam-ni the road first led south up a narrow mountain valley and then turned eastward toward Hagaru-ri. At about the halfway point the road crossed a 4000 foot mountain pass and then descended toward Hagaru-ri. This last section of the road more or less followed the ridge lines and did not offer the same opportunities to the enemy to block the road as did the first part of the road out of Yudam-ni. As events transpired the 7th and 5th did have a hard fight to get up to the pass, but the descent to Hagaru-ri, although opposed, was relatively easier.

During these operations one company of the 7th Marines had a unique and remarkable experience. This was F Company. In his initial advance to Yudam-ni, Litzenberg had left E and F Companies in occupancy of high ground along the road to the rear. Litzenberg was able to extricate E Company, but could not reach F Company which was in position at the top of the mountain. It was completely surrounded but held excellent positions. By pinpoint air drops we were able to keep the company supplied with ammunition and rations. It had 18 killed and 60 wounded but held out for over three days when it was relieved by 1/7 pushing back up the mountain from Yudam-ni.

During the night of November 30th–December 1st Hagaru-ri was again heavily attacked but the perimeter held. We were stronger this time as G Company of 3/1 and the Commandos had joined our defense force. The attacks were from the southwest and the east. The attack from the east fell on the sector manned by the Service Battalion. LtCol Banks, an ex-Raider, was in command of the Service Battalion. He did an excellent job in beating back the attack.

By December 1st the situation with regard to care of casualties was becoming serious. Dr Hering had at Hagaru-ri 600 casualties awaiting evacuation. These were being cared for by C and E Medical Companies. It was estimated 400 casualties would be brought in if the Army battalions east of the reservoir broke out. (Actually we eventually evacuated over 900 men from these battalions). We estimated the 5th and 7th would bring in 500 casualties. (Actually they brought in 1500).

It was manifest that the only solution to our casualty problem was completion of the C-47 strip. (OYs and helicopters could not make a dent in our casualty load.) Our engineers had worked night and day on the C-47 strip. On two nights work had to be interrupted because of enemy attacks and the engineers manned their part of the perimeter near the field. The front lines were only 300 yards from the end of the runway. The strip was rather crude; 3800 feet long, 50 feet wide, no taxiways, and a 2% grade to the north. The soil was black loam but it was frozen. Our equipment had considerable difficulty with the frozen ground. On December 1st the strip, as I have described it, was considered to be 40%

completed, on the advice of the aviators it was decided to bring in a C-47 for a trial run on the afternoon of December 1st. The plane landed successfully at about 1500 and took off 24 wounded. It takes about a half hour to load a plane with litter patients. Ambulatory patients go very much faster. At first we could accommodate only two planes on the ground simultaneously. Eventually, as the field was improved we were able to accommodate six planes on the ground without blocking the runway. Hours of daylight were from about 0700 to 1745 and use of the strip was limited to those hours. After the first plane landed more planes came in. Five additional plane loads of wounded were taken out that afternoon. We would have gotten out more but an incoming plane, loaded with 105mm ammunition collapsed its landing gear. The plane was too heavy, with its load, to push off the runway and we had to unload it, thus losing valuable time. (We attempted to have incoming planes loaded with ammunition and other needed supplies to supplement air drops.)

I will complete the story of evacuation of casualties from Hagaru-ri out of chronology as it is all one story and a very remarkable accomplishment when viewed as a whole. On the evening of December 1st stragglers from the break-up of the Army battalions east of the lake began to drift in. During the day of December 2nd we evacuated 919 casualties by air, the majority of them from the Army battalions. During the morning of December 3d the doctor cleaned out by air evacuation all his remaining casualties. This gave us an opportunity to fly out our accumulation of dead. The estimate of casualties of the 5th and 7th Marines had now risen to 900. At 1935, December 3d, the advance guard of the 7th Marines arrived at the perimeter. It was closely followed by the column of walking wounded. The column continued the movement during the night and each vehicle brought in more wounded, some on the hoods of jeeps. By morning the doctor's hospital installations were full. On the day of December 4th 1000 casualties were evacuated by air. On the day of December 5th 1400 more casualties were evacuated by air. When we moved out from Hagaru-ri to Koto-ri on December 6th we had no remaining casualties to evacuate.

I believe the story of this evacuation is without parallel. Credit must go to the troop commanders whose determination and self-sacrifice made it possible to get the wounded out, to the medical personnel whose devotion to duty and untiring efforts saved many lives, and to the Marine and Air Force [air crews](including fatal accident[s] in spite of the hazards of the weather and a rudimentary landing strip.)

To get back to the story of the operation in its proper chronological sequence. At 1335, December 1st, we got our first air drop from Japan. These drops were known as "Baldwins". Each "Baldwin" contained a prearranged quantity of small arms ammunition, weapons, water, rations, and medical supplies. Artillery ammunition had to be requested separately. A "Baldwin" could be dropped by about six C-119 planes. We were required to make request on Corps for the number of "Baldwins" desired, modified as desired. We usually requested "Baldwins" less weapons and water and plus given quantities of artillery ammunition.

Air drop did not have the capability of supplying a Marine division in combat. When the drops were started the total capability of the Far East Air Force was 70 tons a day. This was stepped up to 100 tons a day. But to support an RCT in combat requires 105 tons a day. What gave us some cushion was the fact that with our own transportation, before the roads were cut, we had built up at Hagaru-ri a level of six days rations and two units of fire. The air drops continued until we left Hagaru-ri and were also made at Koto-ri where Puller had to be supplied and where we had to accumulate supplies in anticipation of the arrival of the bulk of the division there. The drops were not always accurate and we had personnel and materiel casualties as a result of inaccurate drops; however, we owe a considerable debt of gratitude to the Air Force for their efforts.

During the afternoon of December 1st a deputy chief of staff of the Corps arrived and gave me the outline of the latest plan. Under this plan the 3d Infantry Division was to move elements to Majong-dong (about 10 miles south of the foot of the mountain) and establish a covering force through which I would withdraw. Upon withdrawal I was to occupy a defensive sector west and southwest of Hungnam and the 7th Division was to occupy a sector northeast and north of Hungnam.

Toward evening of December 1st some 300 stragglers of the cut off Army battalions up the reservoir drifted into camp, having made their way in over the frozen surface of the reservoir. They continued to drift in during the night and for three or four days thereafter. I have never found out exactly what happened. Apparently the two battalions which had holed up at Sinhung-ni started south and had made some progress, with the support of a considerable amount of Marine aviation (10 planes on either side of the road). Then the acting regimental commander was killed and the column must have fallen apart and men made the best of their way out to the lake and thence down the lake to our perimeter. For some unknown reason the Chinese did not do much firing at people on the surface of the lake. We evacuated some 900 men of the two infantry battalions and artillery battalion. There remained with us some 385 more or less able bodied men whom I had the senior Army officer present form into a provisional battalion. We brought these out with us.

During the day of December 2d LtCol Beall and other volunteers conducted a remarkable rescue operation on the lake: Air cover was provided. They drove jeeps, often towing improvised sleds, as far as four miles over the surface of the reservoir, and picked up wounded and frostbitten men. Although the Chinese did not often fire on the wounded on the lake they did fire at the jeeps. During the day 250 men were rescued by these jeeps. Operations were continued the following day but a lesser number were found. Beall was awarded the DSC by the Corps Commander.

The 5th and 7th made some progress up the mountain during December 2d. Enemy opposition was still strong.

On December 3d Litzenberg reached the top of the mountain between Yudam-ni and Hagaru-ri. However, there was still a buildup of enemy between him and us and he was running short of gasoline. In a slow-moving column there is considerable idling of motors and in any event, in cold weather, motors have to be started up frequently. All this consumes a large quantity of gasoline. At Litzenberg's request we made a pinpoint drop of gasoline to the head of the truck column. Unfortunately, he did not request diesel fuel, a lack of which later was responsible for the loss of several artillery pieces.

During the day of December 3d Litzenberg continued to push over and down the mountain. At 1630 we sent out tanks with the Commandos to clean out the Chinese who were on the road near camp. At 1935 the advance guard of the 7th Marines arrived at the perimeter. Movement continued during the night, the 5th Marines following in after the 7th. In the darkness it takes a long time to get units in from covering positions and on to the road. When they were only a few miles from Hagaru-ri some of the tractors drawing the 155mm howitzers ran out of diesel fuel. This stopped the column. The Chinese closed in with mortar and automatic weapon fire. Some of the tractors were disabled. We later sent a column back with diesel fuel, but not all the guns could be gotten out because of disabled tractors. We lost 10 out of 18 155mm howitzers and 4 out of 30 105mm howitzers. The guns were spiked and later an air strike was put down on them. Despite the losses it was still a remarkable feat to bring out three battalions of artillery minus these guns.

The last elements of the 5th and 7th Marines did not arrive at Hagaru-ri until about noon of December 4th. I was considerably relieved to have these two regiments rejoin. I considered that the critical part of the operation had been completed. Even with two depleted RCTs I felt confident we could fight our way to Koto-ri where we would gain additional strength. The terrain was not as difficult, it lent itself well to air support, and we were able to lay down preparatory artillery fires all the way to Koto-ri. Artillery emplaced at Hagaru-ri could reach half way to Koto-ri and Puller's artillery at Koto-ri could reach back to meet our fires.

After their grueling experience the regiments were not in condition to continue the advance on December 5th. Also we wanted to be sure that all our casualties were evacuated. Our order, therefore, provided for an advance on Koto-ri at first light on December 6th.

The order for the advance on Koto-ri provided for an advance in two RCT columns. RCT 7 led out. The RCT was normal as to combat troops, with the provisional Army battalion attached. In addition, Litzenberg had within his column his own regimental train and Division Train No. l. RCT 5 was to follow RCT 7o Its composition was normal except for the attachment of 3/l. Murray also had within his column his own regimental train and Division Train No. 2. He was to hold the perimeter until RCT 7 had gained sufficient distance to permit him to move out on the road.

The embarrassing part of this move was the trains. Over a thousand vehicles were involved. We carried two days rations and two units of fire. We brought out all usable equipment and supplies, including tentage and stoves. Even the engineer pans were used as trucks to carry tentage.

Litzenberg had not advanced more than two miles before he ran into trouble. Using maximum air and artillery support it required until 1400 to break through. Peculiarly enough all the opposition came from the east side of the road.

At 1420 I moved my operational CP by OY plane and helicopter to Koto-ri. My radios, vans and working personnel were mostly in Division Train No. l.

By 1800, December 6th Litzenberg had reached the halfway point and was progressing satisfactorily. However, during the night the Chinese cut into the train in two places.

There was confused and close range fighting. We lost men and vehicles but remarkably few vehicles.

The column continued to move during the night and by 0590, December 7th, the leading elements of the 7th Marines began to arrive at Koto-ri.

The 5th Marines did not clear Hagaru-ri until December 7th. Murray had quite a rear guard action at that place, but came off with 200 prisoners. His last elements did not close Koto-ri until 2135, December 7th.

The advance from Hagaru-ri to Koto-ri cost us more than 500 casualties. Puller had an OY strip only. However, Field Harris agreed to land TBM planes, of which he had three, on this strip. During the day of December 7th, between OYs and TBMs, 200 casualties were evacuated. However, there were still 300 more casualties to evacuate. The aviators stated that if 400 feet was added to the strip it would be possible for C-47s to land. Therefore, during the night of December 7–8, our engineers lengthened the strip by 400 feet. Unfortunately, the strip was periodically under enemy fire. On December 8th C-47s began to land and we soon completed evacuation of our casualties.

Koto-ri is about two miles north of the lip of the mountain. From the lip of the mountain the road descends tortuously to Chinhung-ni about 10 road miles distant. At Chinhung-ni was Puller's 1st Battalion. On December 7th the Corps had moved an Army battalion to Chinhung-ni in order to free l/l. Theoretically, the road was open from Chinhung-ni to the south.

Our plan for getting down the mountain was simple. (However, it must be borne in mind that the enemy surrounded Koto-ri as they had closed in behind our columns.) The 5th and 7th Marines were to seize and hold the commanding ground to about the half way point. 1/1 was to push up from Chinhung-ni and seize and hold commanding ground about half way up the mountain. The 1st Marines, which had regained 3/1 from Hagaru-ri and additionally had a battalion of the 31st Infantry attached, was to hold the perimeter at Koto-ri until the trains cleared when it was to follow auto (We now had 1400 vehicles as a result of the addition of Puller's train and Army vehicles). Once the commanding ground was seized it was our intention to push the trains down the mountain. As the trains cleared, infantry would leave the high ground and move down the road. The last vehicles in the column were the tanks. We realized that if an M-26 ever stalled or threw a tread on a one-way mountain road it would be very difficult to clear it out of the way.

In all this planning there was one serious catch. The Chinese had blown out a twenty-four foot section of a bridge about a third of the way down the mountain. They could not have picked a better spot to cause us serious trouble. At this point four large pipes, carrying water to the turbines of the power plant in the valley below crossed the road. A sort of concrete substation was built over the pipes on the uphill side of the road. A one-way concrete bridge went around the substation. The drop down the mountainside was sheer. It was a section of this bridge which was blown. There was no possibility of a by-pass.

Partridge, our engineer, got together with the commanding officer of a Treadway Bridge unit which was stranded at Koto-ri and they devised a plan. This involved dropping by parachute at Koto-ri the necessary Treadway Bridge sections. These were dropped on December 7th. As a precaution additional sections were spotted at Chinhung-ni at the foot of the mountain.

At 0800 on December 8th, the 7th Marines jumped off to seize Objectives A and B at the lip of the mountain; then it pushed on to Objective C further along. The 5th moved out and captured Objective D above the bridge site. 1/1 moved up the mountain and captured Objective E. All this was not accomplished as easily as it is described. There were delays and casualties. The bridging material did not get to the bridge site until December 9th. The bridge was

This blown bridge at Funchilin Pass blocked the only way out for U.S. and British forces withdrawing from the Chosin Reservoir. Air Force C-119 Flying Boxcars dropped portable bridge sections to span the chasm in December 1950. These were assembled by Marine and Army combat engineers and they allowed men and equipment to continue through the pass. (Official USAF photograph)

completed at 1615 that date. In anticipation of completion of the bridge the truck column had been moved forward and the leading truck was ready to cross as soon as the bridge was completed. Unfortunately, another block developed further down the mountain where the road passed under the cableway. This block was caused partly by enemy fire and partly by additional demolition. This block was not opened until 0600, December 10th.

What we had feared regarding the tanks occurred. As I explained previously we had placed them last in the column. As they were proceeding down the mountain the brake on the seventh tank from the tail of the column locked. The tank jammed into the bank. Efforts to bypass the tank or push it out of the way were fruitless. To complicate matters the Chinese closed in with mortar fire and thermite grenades and mingled with the crowds of refugees following the column. The tankers dismounted and fought on foot with the Reconnaissance Company which was covering the tail of the column. There were Casualties. Finally the tankers did their best to disable the seven tanks and moved down the mountain. Next morning an air strike was put in on the tanks as well as the bridge which we had laboriously constructed.

During the day of December 10th both Division Trains Nos. 1 and 2 cleared Chinhung-ni at the foot of the mountain and leading elements of the trains began arriving at Hamhung that afternoon. After the trains cleared the road, empty trucks were sent up for troops.

At 1300, December 11th, the last elements of the division cleared Chinhung-ni. The 3d Division was supposed to keep the road open south of Chinhung-ni, but Puller's regimental train was ambushed near Sudong. He lost a couple of trucks and had some casualties. However, Puller arrived at his assembly area with more vehicles than he had started down the mountain with. He had picked up and towed in some vehicles he had found at the scene of a previous ambush of Army trucks. Puller's last elements arrived in the assembly area at 2100, December 11th. This completed the move of the division from the Chosin Reservoir area.

Our rear echelon had set up 150 tents with stoves for each regiment. Hot food was available when the troops arrived.

While Puller was closing his assembly area on December 11th, the 7th Marines was embarking in the MSTS *Daniel I. Sultan*. The 5th Marines embarked December 12th and the 1st Marines on December 13th. Loading out of the division was completed about midnight December 14th, and the last ship of the convoy sailed at 1030, December 15th.

An approximation of the casualties from the date (November 27th) we jumped off in the attack to the westward until we returned to Hungnam (December 11th) is as follows:

KIA	400
WIA	2265
MIA	90
Total Battle	2755
Non-Battle	1395 (Mostly frostbite)
Grand Total	4150

This is not the complete picture as there are many more frost-bite cases which are now being screened.

I am understandably proud of the performance of this Division. The officers and men were magnificent. They came down the mountains bearded, footsore, and physically exhausted, but their spirits were high. They were still a fighting division.

During the Korean War the Marine Corps first tested the concept of moving troops via helicopter. Here a Sikorski HRS-1 helicopter of Marine Helicopter Transport Squadron 161 (HMR-16) provides foxhole relief with a fresh load of replacements for the 1st Marine Division at an advance base in Korea, November 22, 1951. The troop drop was near the front lines while Marine Corsair fighter-bombers furnished air support to keep enemy guns quiet on a nearby hill position. (Official USMC photograph)

During the two and a half years that followed the Chosin Reservoir fighting, the 1st Marine Division and the 1st Marine Aircraft Wing fought as a part of EUSAK, not as an amphibious force, but as part of a land army. The Marines were assigned missions similar to Army divisions, and aviation elements were placed under overall control of the Air Force.

Then Second Lieutenant Petersen climbs from his Corsair fighter bomber at a base of the 1st Marine Aircraft Wing in Korea, April 19, 1953. (Official USMC photograph)

A helicopter troop landing during the Korean War pointed the way towards the Corps' increased relevance as a strategically mobile naval infantry force, capable of responding to a wide variety of situations as needed by the nation at short notice. Working closely with the Navy, the Corps remained ready to provide power projection ashore for the fleet.

The Chosin campaign was arguably the Corps' greatest moment as a fighting force. Throughout the war the Marines added greatly to the fierce reputation they had earned on the beaches of the Pacific. Father Kevin Keaney, 1st Marine Division Chaplain, summed it up well. "You cannot exaggerate about the Marines. They are convinced to the point of arrogance, that they are the most ferocious fighters on earth—and the amusing thing about it is that they are."

CHAPTER 5

COLD WAR CONTINGENCY FORCE, 1954–1980

World War II and the Korean War established the Marine Corps as one of the world's elite fighting forces. Dedicated to its amphibious warfare mission as well as being the nation's "First to Fight," it had unquestionably become the preferred "ready force" available for deployment by the president at a moment's notice. Additionally, the National Security Act of 1947 provided the Marine Corps with long-needed statuary protection; its existence had finally been enshrined in law. However, this could not protect the Corps from budget cuts or the possibility of operational irrelevance in the nuclear age.

The Cold War that began in earnest after 1948 introduced new geopolitical realities that required the Marine Corps to rethink its doctrines and concepts. On the one hand, the Corps needed to be prepared to support the global needs of the Navy with ready amphibious forces while on the other it needed to find a place for itself within the framework of the North Atlantic Treaty Organization's war plans. Doctrinally, this demanded the continual refinement of air-ground task force organization developed over the decades and the hurried adoption of evolving technologies that would allow the Corps to maintain its expeditionary edge and naval mindset.

Prior to World War I the Marine Corps focused on individual marksmanship, and gave Marines extra pay for qualifying as rifle experts. Marine marksmanship became legendary. In this image Marine recruits at San Diego Recruit Depot are taught how to shoot the Marine way at the mid-range, 300-yard line on at Camp Matthews with Platoons 13 and 156, February 14, 1952. (Official USMC photograph)

This steady evolution continued during one of the most dynamic periods of the Marine Corps' history, even as it supported the Army in the decade-long Vietnam War, which spanned the spectrum from traditional counterinsurgency warfare to large-scale conventional operations. To successfully fight this increasingly unpopular kind of war, the Corps drew on its experiences from World War II and the Banana Wars, testimony to its flexibility and willingness to adapt to arising challenges.

As its techniques and tactics evolved to insure that the Corps would remain relevant and effective in the changing military-technological environment of the 20th century, it was also perfecting its ability to make Marines. Following "a form of unfailing alchemy," as Lieutenant General Victor H. Krulak describes it in his polemic, *First to Fight: An Inside View of the U.S. Marine Corps* (1984), drill instructors transformed the young men and women of character who arrived at Parris Island, San Diego, or Quantico into Marines, "whose hands the nation's affairs may safely be entrusted." Despite this fabled alchemy, making Marines has never been easy for the Corps. Incidents such as the notorious Ribbon Creek, South Carolina tragedy in 1956 illustrated that the service can never take the process of making Marines for granted. Doing so requires constant refinement and attention. With the end of selective service and rising racial tensions in the wake of the Vietnam War, the decade of the 1970s introduced new challenges into the process of making Marines.

In July 1958, a brigade-size force landed in Lebanon to restore order there. During the Cuban Missile Crisis in October 1962, a large amphibious force was marshaled but not landed. Thirty months later, in April 1965, a brigade of Marine landed in the Dominican Republic to protect Americans and evacuate those who wished to leave.

The landing of the 9th Marine Expeditionary Brigade (9th MEB) at Da Nang in 1965 marked the beginning of large-scale Marine involvement in Vietnam. Although initially ordered that they would "not, repeat, will not, engage in day-to-day actions against the Viet Cong" it did not take long for the Marines' mission to transform into large-scale counterinsurgency operations. By May, 1965 the 9th MEB turned into the III Marine Amphibious Force (III MAF) to include elements of the 3d Marine Division and the 1st Marine Aircraft Wing. Within a few months, elements of the 1st Marine Division had joined III MAF as well.

1968 was arguably the busiest year of the Vietnam War, especially for the Marine Corps which faced the onslaught of the Tet Offensive, fought major battles at Hue City and Khe Sanh, along with numerous skirmishes and continued the counterinsurgency mission throughout the I Corps Tactical Zone. Tet captured the world's attention, but the bloodiest month of the war for the U.S. forces came in May 1968. The intensity of conflict across I Corps in 1968 is amply illustrated by the 11 Marines and two Navy Corpsmen who were awarded the Medal of Honor for actions during the year. Through hard fighting, Marines and allied forces in the I Corps tactical zone regained the offensive but a turning point had been reached— American participation in the war would not continue forever.

At the start of 1968, III MAF controlled the I Corps tactical zone, comprised of the five northern provinces of the Republic of Vietnam. Over 100,000 Marines, sailors, and soldiers served there, including the 1st and 3d Marine Divisions, the 1st Marine Aircraft Wing, the Force Logistics Command, the 23d Infantry Division, the Seventh Fleet's Special Landing Force, and the Republic of Korea's 2d Marine Brigade. This large, combined, joint force was commanded by Lieutenant General Robert E. Cushman but command relationships were byzantine. Ultimately Cushman reported to General William C. Westmoreland, commanding general of the U.S. Military Assistance Command—Vietnam (MACV) but also reported administratively to Lieutenant General Victor H. Krulak of Fleet Marine Forces—Pacific and General Wallace M. Greene, commandant of the Marine Corps (General Leonard F. Chapman replaced Greene on January 31). In the pre-Goldwater-Nichols era such relationships were even more fraught with tension then they are today.

The Marine Corps began 1968 with the 3d Marine Division largely strung out along the eastern DMZ in primarily fixed positions. The 5th Marines concluded Operation *Auburn* south of Da Nang, working with Army of the Republic of Vietnam (ARVN) battalions in the sort of offensive sweep which was designed to clear given locations of enemy guerrilla forces. The 2d Battalion, 26th Marines reinforced the Marine base at Khe Sanh.

On January 20, three months of long operations concluded: the 3d Marines concluded Operation *Lancaster I* on Route 9 between Cam Lo and Ca Lu, the 1st Marines concluded Operation *Osceola I* in the Quang Tri City region, and the 4th Marines concluded Operation Neosho I northwest of Hue. And a Marine patrol on Hill 881 South near Khe Sanh ran into a large North Vietnamese force, the first action in the siege of Khe Sanh. The next day the 1st Air Cavalry Division, U.S. Army, was placed under the operational control of III MAF. The 4th Marines began Operation *Lancaster II* and the 3d Marines began Operation *Osceola II* in the same area as their prequel operations. The North Vietnamese Army began the bombardment of Khe Sanh and its outposts that would continue for the next 77 days. The Special Landing Force and 1st Amphibian Tractor Battalion worked to keep the Cua Viet River supply line open with Operation *Napoleon* (later renamed Saline).

Even as the North Vietnamese and the Marines continued to struggle for the Khe Sanh, the rest of South Vietnam prepared for the Tet holiday and the hoped-for cease-fire, but on January 30 the Tet Offensive began in I Corps. On January 31, the Tet Offensive spread throughout South Vietnam. The aim of the communist forces was to spur a broad, major uprising in South Vietnam to destabilize its government. The most high-profile assault on the U.S. Embassy in Saigon failed after breaching the compound.

The fighting was fierce but brief across most of the country as American and South Vietnamese forces put down the uprisings. But in the Vietnamese Imperial City of Hue the North

Vietnamese clung to their gains, massacring locals, fortifying their positions, and forcing the allied forces to clear them from the palace and surrounding city through intense, block by block fighting.

Fourteen enemy battalions had been assembled for the assault, and between 15 to 18 battalions would take part in the battle before it was over. The city of Hue was in the northern end of South Vietnam situated along the Huong River. The city was the intellectual and religious center of Vietnam as well as being the former imperial capital. Hue was divided into two sections. North of the Huong river was the Imperial City which was dominated by the Citadel, a massive-walled fortress which had been modeled after the Forbidden City in China. The southern section of Hue was a modern and bustling municipality with buildings in the European and American style. The city was relatively lightly defended by American and South Vietnamese forces.

On January 31, the NVA and Vietcong swept through Hue, taking all but two holdout areas, one on each side of the river. In the Citadel the commander of the South Vietnamese 1st Infantry Division, General Truong, was able to beat off enemy attacks and hold on to his headquarters in the Mang Ca compound. Similarly, in the southern city, the personnel of the MACV compound fought off the NVA attacks long enough to be relieved. A Company, 1st Battalion, 1st Marines, and G Company, 2d Battalion, 5th Marines, reinforced with four tanks from the 3d Tank Battalion, fought their way to the MACV compound, ensuring it remained in American hands. These Marines then attempted to assault across the Nguyen Hoang Bridge but pulled back after suffering heavy casualties.

Beginning on February 1, the 1st ARVN Division was ordered to retake the Citadel while the Marines' Task Force X-Ray fought for the southern city. Two Marine companies launched an attack toward the provincial building and prison. Meanwhile, north of the river, 1st ARVN Division was able to recapture Tay Loc Airfield. On February 2 the Army's 3d Brigade, 1st Cavalry

Marines of H Company, 2d Battalion, 5th Marines, cover a blown wall during fighting in Hue City. (Official USMC photograph)

Division launched an attack southeast towards Hue to cut off enemy supply lines but their attack was badly mauled. The Marines in the city were reinforced, H Company, 2/5 having to fight through an enemy ambush to reach the MACV compound. "The compound reminded me of an old fort surrounded by Indians," the commander of H Company, Captain Christmas, said. After a three-hour fight the reinforced Marines were able to reach the Hue University Campus, but when a tank was hit they were ordered to withdraw back to their MACV positions. That night the NVA dropped the railroad bridge across the Perfume River on the west side of the city but the bridge across the Phu Cam Canal was left untouched.

From February 3–8 the Marines fought a savage, block-by-block urban fight with the Vietnamese Communists fighting to hold the city, utilizing strongpoints and defending every other street. One Marine described the situation as "like fighting a hive of bees. Fire was coming from street level, from windows on the second floor and from the roof of every building. We had to crawl everywhere and then call in the tanks so we could retrieve our wounded."

Eight days into the fight for Hue City, on February 6, 1968, Marines of 2d Battalion, 5th Marines captured the provincial headquarters in southern Hue City after fierce fighting. The headquarters had stood as a symbol throughout the battle, a Viet Cong National Liberation Front flag flew in its courtyard. A television crew from CBS was on hand to film it as two Marines took down the Viet Cong flag and a third, Gunnery Sergeant Frank A. Thomas, raised the United States flag in its place. After the fierce fighting of the previous eight days, Captain George R. Christmas ignored the standing order to only raise the national colors alongside the flag of the Republic of South Vietnam. Marine combat correspondent Sergeant Stephen Berntson interviewed Christmas after the flag raising, his notes from that interview highlighting how the Marines saw the flag raising that day. He said it was the most "inspirational thing I have ever seen in my lifetime—because it was a hard thing. That feeling of patriotism … all you could hear are cheers … really brings out American spirit." However, taking the provincial headquarters was not merely symbolic, it was the headquarters for the 4th NVA Regiment, and the result was that after its capture the Communist forces in the city were no longer able to coordinate their defenses.

By February 10 the southern sector of the city was in Marine hands but the Citadel was still largely controlled by the NVA. By February 13, Marine engineers had built a pontoon bridge alongside the destroyed An Cuu span allowing for the flow of supplies to Marines and civilians alike to resume.

While the Marines were successfully clearing out the southern city, the fighting in the Citadel was reduced to a stalemate. The NVA had fortified hundreds of strong stone structures creating a series of defensive lines composed of interconnected strong points and were able to move reinforcements into the Citadel at night.

On February 11 and 12, 1st Battalion, 5th Marines was airlifted inside the Mang Ca compound. On February 13, 1/5 moved out with five tanks in support to continue the attack on the Citadel. They were met with fierce enemy resistance from heavily fortified positions from the outset. On February 15, after a ferocious six-hour fight, they captured a tower on the east wall of the Citadel. One Marine company commander described the fighting. "I had to admire the courage and discipline of the North Vietnamese and the Viet Cong, but no more than my own men. We were both in a face-to-face, eyeball-to-eyeball confrontation. Sometimes they were only twenty or thirty yards from us, and once we killed a sniper only ten yards away. After a while, survival was the name of the game as you sat there in the semidarkness, with the firing going on constantly…. And the horrible smell. You tasted it as you ate your rations, as if you were eating death. It permeated your clothes, which you couldn't wash because water was very scarce…. My strategy was to keep as many of my Marines alive as possible, and yet accomplish the mission. You went through the full range of emotions, seeing your buddies being hit, buy you couldn't feel sorry for them because you had others to think about. It was dreary, and still we weren't depressed. We were doing our job—successfully."

Day after day the Marines fought inch by inch through the Citadel alongside their South Vietnamese allies. The Marines, who had been accustomed to jungle warfare, rapidly readjusted to urban tactics. After heavy fighting, a temporary halt to the advance was called on 17 February. Marine numbers were heavily depleted at this point in the battle. One officer remarked "We don't have enough men, enough air support, or enough artillery to do this thing quickly…." Poor weather ensured that air support was only available on three days of the fight for the Citadel, 14 to 16 February. The Citadel was defended steadfastly by committed enemy forces and on 18 February the North Vietnamese troops were ordered to "remain in position and fight." The Citadel itself was designed for defense, with limited access ways and fighting positions dug along its wall.

Marines of C Company, 1st Battalion, 5th Regiment engaged in a fire fight in streets of Hue during Operation Hue City. *Most of the fighting in the Vietnam War took place in rural areas, and often involved patrols, snipers, and ambushes with a seldom-seen enemy. The battle for Hue was one of the exceptions as the Marines fought a vicious, block-by-block urban battle with the Vietnamese Communists. (Official USMC photograph)*

Troops from the Army's 1st Cavalry and 101st Airborne divisions sealed off the city, preventing further communist reinforcements, on February 21. From that point things turned against the communists and resistance in the Citadel became desperate. Early the next morning, Marines launched a successful night attack and then continued to push forward as enemy resistance melted. On the morning of February 22, 1st Battalion, 5th Marines reached the southern wall of the Citadel at the heart of the Imperial city. According to the battalion's after action report, Lance Corporal James Avella took a small American flag from his pack and fastened it to "a sagging telegraph pole." The report documented this event with the phrase, an "element" of Company A "hoisted our National Ensign." The Marines' fight in the Citadel was over.

The Citadel, the fortress at the heart of the Imperial city, had been held by the Communists since the first day of the

Large clouds of dust and smoke obscure part of the Khe Sanh Combat Base after an enemy rocket and artillery bombardment. On February 23, a Marine ammunition supply point took a direct hit, which resulted in several secondary explosions. Despite the daily shelling, the Vietnamese never seriously threatened the base. (Official USMC photograph)

offensive. Throughout a red-starred, blue-and-white-striped Vietcong flag had flown on the platform before the Ngo Mon gate, announcing the communists' success and perseverance to the world. Most of the fighting for the Citadel was performed by South Vietnamese forces, supported by American artillery, armor, and air strikes. Its recapture on February 24, after weeks of fierce urban fighting was a dramatic moment, one that the men of the 212th Company, 3d ARVN Regiment seized when they raised the South Vietnamese flag at the Ngo Mon gate of the Citadel. The failure in Vietnam of the Tet Offensive could not have been better illustrated.

Elsewhere in I Corps, the 26th Marines at Khe Sanh repelled a battalion-sized attack, but the Special Forces base at Lang Vei, west of Khe Sanh, was over run. 5th Marines and the Americal Division fought off the 2d North Vietnamese Division around Da Nang. Even as American and South Vietnamese forces liberated the Citadel and declared the city of Hue secure, the heaviest shelling of the siege occurred at Khe Sanh.

The daily shelling certainly established a routine at Khe Sanh. During the siege on Hill 881 South, each morning the Marines began their day the same way, as Captain Moyers S. Shore II, USMC, relates in *The Battle for Khe Sanh*, 1977:

"Attention to Colors." The order having been given, Captain William H. Dabney, a product of the Virginia Military Institute, snapped to attention, faced the jerry-rigged flagpole, and saluted, as did every other man in Company I, 3d Battalion, 26th Marines. The ceremony might well have been at any one of a hundred military installations around the world except for a few glaring irregularities. The parade ground was a battle-scarred hilltop to the west of Khe Sanh and the men in the formation stood half submerged in trenches or foxholes. Instead of crisply starched utilities, razor sharp creases, and gleaming brass, these Marines sported scraggly beards, ragged trousers, and rotted helmet liner straps. The only man in the company who could play a bugle, Second Lieutenant Owen S. Matthews, lifted the pock-marked instrument to his lips and spat out a choppy version of "To the Colors" while two enlisted men raced to the RC-292 radio antenna which served as the flagpole and gingerly attached the Stars and Stripes. As the mast with its shredded banner came upright, the Marines could hear the ominous "thunk," "thunk," "thunk," to the southwest of their position which meant that North Vietnamese 120mm mortar rounds had left their tubes. They also knew that in 21 seconds those "thunks" would be replaced by much louder, closer sounds but no one budged until Old Glory waved high over the hill.

When Lieutenant Matthews sharply cut off the last note of his piece, Company I disappeared; men dropped into trenches, dived headlong into foxholes, or scrambled into bunkers. The area which moments before had been bristling with humanity was suddenly a ghost town. Seconds later explosions walked across the hilltop spewing black smoke, dirt, and debris into the air. Rocks, splinters, and spent shell fragments rained on the flattened Marines but, as usual, no one was hurt. As quickly as the attack came, it was over. While the smoke lazily drifted away, a much smaller banner rose from the Marines' positions. A pole adorned with a pair of red, silk panties—Maggie's Drawers*—was waved back and forth above one trenchline to inform the enemy that he had missed again. A few men stood up and jeered or cursed at the distant gunners; others simply saluted with an appropriate obscene gesture. The daily flag-raising ceremony on Hill 881 South was over.

In March the Provisional Corps Vietnam was created, answering to Lieutenant General Cushman. This command, led by Lieutenant General William B. Rosson, USA, controlled the 3d Marine Division, the 1st Air Cavalry Division, and the 101st Airborne Division and was subordinate to Lieutenant General Cushman, commander of III MAF. Operation *Scotland*, which began in November 1967 and included the defense of Khe Sanh, ended.

April began with the 1st Air Cavalry Division, together with units from the 1st Marines and the ARVN, executing Operation *Pegasus*, reopening the land route to the Marine garrison at Khe Sanh, retaking the camp at Lang Vei on April 9, declaring Route 9 open on April 11, and ending successfully in the middle of April. Marines immediately began Operation *Scotland II* around the base at Khe Sanh.

In May the counterattack continued across I Corps. The 7th Marines began Operation *Allen Brook* south of Da Nang. Communist rocket and mortar attacks across South Vietnam began their second major offensive of the year. In the middle of the month, the 1st Air Cavalry Division began Operation *Jeb Stuart III* in Quang Tri and Thua Thien, while the 1st Marine

---

* Maggie's Drawers is a slang term that refers to the flag waved at the rifle range when a shooter has completely missed the target.

Division began Operation *Mameluke Thrust* in Quang Nam, attempting to disrupt an expected enemy offensive.

The Marines dismantled and withdrew from Khe Sanh combat base in June, as Operation *Kentucky*, which had begun in November 1967, continued along the DMZ.

At the start of July, General Creighton Abrams relieved General William Westmoreland as Commander USMACV. Along the DMZ, Marine, Air Force, and Navy aircraft joined with Army and Marine artillery and naval gunfire from cruisers and destroyers off the coast to destroy enemy artillery installations in the Demilitarized Zone during the week-long Operation *Thor*. On August 23 the communists mounted a third major offensive, with a major thrust at the city of Da Nang.

In the first half of October, the 7th Marines conducted Operation *Maui Peak* in Quang Nam province. On October 23, Operation *Mameluke Thrust* concluded. The 5th Marines began Operation *Henderson Hill* in the Quang Nam province. At the end of the month, the 1st Air Cavalry Division left I Corps and President Johnson announced a complete halt in the bombing and naval bombardment of North Vietnam.

On November 20, the 1st Marines began Operation *Meade River*, south of Da Nang, in support of the South Vietnamese Accelerated Pacification Campaign. The 4th Marines concluded Operation *Lancaster II*, begun in January.

On December 6, the 5th Marines concluded Operation *Henderson Hill*, begun in October. Then Operation *Napoleon/Saline*, the effort to keep the Cua Viet River supply line open, ended, as did Operation *Meade River*.

1968 ended with the Marines reported to have inflicted 31,691 enemy casualties. The Corps lost 4,618 Marines killed and suffered 29,320 wounded. The Marines had won two of the largest conventional battles of the war at Hue City and Khe Sanh, and then shifted from defending the obstacle system along the DMZ to large mobile operations throughout I Corps. Greater changes for the Marine in Vietnam were to come after 1968 with new strategies and a new presidential administration.

Marines from the 2d Battalion, 3d Marines examine a landing zone on Mutters Ridge as a Marine UH-1E helicopter sits nearby. The Marines made great use of helicopter mobility during the war in Vietnam. (Official USMC photograph)

Following 1968, Marines fought in multiple operations throughout the I Corps area but they successfully transitioned the war to South Vietnamese control in 1971, when the III Marine Amphibious Corps was pulled from Vietnam. Many Marines remained in Vietnam for two more years as advisors, however, fighting alongside the South Vietnamese against the 1972 Easter offensive.

In July 1974 Marines aided in the evacuation of U.S. citizens and foreign nationals during the unrest on Cyprus. The following year saw Marines evacuating embassy staffs and American citizens in Phnom Penh, Cambodia and Saigon, Republic of Vietnam. Later, in May 1975, Marines played an integral role in the rescue of the crew of the SS *Mayaguez* captured off the coast of Cambodia.

Like the rest of the U.S. military, the Marines faced difficulties with drugs and race in the aftermath of the Vietnam War and the end of the draft. But the Corps' reputation and *esprit de corps* helped it to overcome these issues, and their successful recruiting campaigns continued to attract a high class of recruit.

Lieutenant General Frank E. Petersen Jr. was born in 1932. Inspired by the death of Ensign Jesse L. Brown, the first African-American naval aviator, in Korea, Petersen entered the Naval Aviation Cadet Program in 1951 and was commissioned in the Marine Corps in 1952. He was the first African-American Marine aviator.

He flew F4U Corsairs with Marine Fighter Squadron 212 (VMF-212) during the Korean War and F-4 Phantoms as the commanding officer of Marine Fighter Attack Squadron 314 (VMFA-314) during the Vietnam War. He was shot down by ground fire in 1968, but quickly returned to duty. He received numerous awards, including the Legion of Merit with Combat "V," Distinguished Flying Cross, and Purple Heart. When he took command of VMFA-314 in 1968, Petersen was the first African-American to command a Marine squadron. In *Into the Tiger's Jaw* (1998), Petersen said:

> Once I found out what being a United States Marine was all about, jumping into the tiger's jaw was just something to do. We'd been trained for combat. That's our reason for being. When the time comes, hell, stick out your can. Let's go. Let's see what that old tiger's got. Let's jump right into his big, old jaw.

After the Vietnam War Lieutenant General Petersen commanded a Marine Aircraft Group, a Marine Amphibious Brigade, and a Marine Aircraft Wing. When he retired in 1988 he was Commanding General, Marine Corps Combat Development Command. He was the "Silver Hawk" of Marine aviation and the "Grey Eagle" of naval aviation as the senior designated aviator (his designation as an aviator preceded all aviators in then the Army and Air Force).

CHAPTER 6

AMERICA'S 911 FORCE, 1980–PRESENT

In the 1980s the Marine Corps continued the process of reinventing itself, bringing new weapons systems and doctrines into operation while still demonstrating the Corps' continued relevance to the national command authority. The Marine Air Ground Task Force was fully integrated into American strategic thinking, with Marine Expeditionary Units serving in the Pacific and the Mediterranean aboard amphibious ready groups as a strategic reserve that the United States president could call on quickly to respond to various types of international crises. Marine air-ground task forces were called upon to intervene militarily in Panama and Grenada, participate in numerous humanitarian missions, and act as peacekeepers in Beirut and Somalia. They proved particularly adept at one of the Corps' oldest responsibilities, protecting Americans caught overseas in a disaster.

Developed following World War II in response to lessons learned in that conflict, the **Marine Air Ground Task Force (MAGTF)** was the Corps' first choice for operational expeditionary units. A flexible, combined-arms formation, the MAGTF has four components and comes in three standard sizes.

Each MAGTF has a command and control element (the MAGTF headquarters), an air combat element, a ground combat element, and a logistics element.

Each of the standard sized MAGTFs have permanent headquarters and staff. The smallest MAGTF is the Marine Expeditionary Unit (MEU) and today there are seven permanent MEUs, three based on each coast and one in Japan. Commanded by a colonel, this regimental sized-unit comprises the MEU headquarters, a Battalion Landing Team (an infantry battalion with an artillery battery, amphibious assault vehicle platoon, combat engineer platoon, light armored reconnaissance company, tank platoon, and reconnaissance platoon), a composite squadron (medium tilt-rotor aircraft squadron with detachments of light, attack, and heavy helicopters as well as VSTOL fixed wing aircraft), and a combat logistic battalion. MEUs are carried aboard a Navy amphibious ready group (now, an expeditionary strike group) and since the 1950s the Marines have generally maintained two MEUs at sea, one in the Mediterranean and one in the Pacific, as the nation's on call expeditionary force.

The next size up is the Marine Expeditionary Brigade (MEB). Commanded by a brigadier general, MEBs are employed when a significant combined-arms force is required. Each has a Brigade headquarters, a regimental landing team (a Marine regiment supported by artillery battalion and armor, light armored reconnaissance, and amphibious assault companies), a Marine Air Group (with fixed wing and helicopter squadrons), and a combat logistics regiment.

The largest MAGTF is the Marine Expeditionary Force. The MEF is commanded by a major general, and is a corps-sized force. It comprises a large MEF headquarters, a Marine division, a Marine Air Wing, and a Marine logistics group. MEFs are employed when a major combat element is needed; the Marine Corps has three permanently staffed MEFs, one on each coast and one in Japan.

The Goldwaters-Nichols Act of 1986 combined the warfighting forces of the United States closer than ever before, creating new theater combatant commands alongside the traditional European and Pacific theater commands. At the same time increased emphasis on the dangers of Soviet aggression against the North Atlantic Treaty Organization under President Ronald Reagan pushed the Corps to training in mountain and arctic environments and joint training with the Norwegians. The creation of the Maritime Prepositioning Program expanded the Corps' ability to project power globally more quickly than ever before.

In 1991 the Corps mobilized over two-thirds of its forces for the Gulf War under the umbrella of the I Marine Expeditionary Force. The new weapons systems and doctrine were tried under battle conditions as the new training systems and the Marines of the post-draft Corps were put to the test. The Iraqi military was far from a first-class opponent, but the performance of the Corps in the Gulf remained impressive, and all of the major new systems worked as expected or better. The United States enjoyed multiple benefits of amphibious power as it led a nearly global coalition in opposition to Iraq's August 1990 invasion and occupation of Kuwait. At every step, from the defense of Saudi Arabia to the liberation of Kuwait, amphibious power enabled American success.

The 1980s were a time of **intellectual renaissance in the United States military**, especially the Marine Corps. Determined to fix deficiencies they felt had crept into doctrine and equipment, the Marine Corps developed the AV-8B Harrier and the AH-1W Super Cobra alongside the CH-53 to enhance its expeditionary airfield concept. It added the Light Armored Vehicle to its inventory, creating new battalions to field these versatile vehicles which were armed with 25mm chain guns, TOW missiles, or mortars, and carried fire teams of infantry Marines as well. The Corps replaced its aging M-60 tanks with modern M1A1 Abrams. The most high profile bit of equipment development was the MV-22 Osprey, a tilt rotor aircraft which allowed the transport of Marines at great speed over range.

All of these weapons systems were in service to the Corps' new "maneuver warfare" doctrine, as Marines were focused on fighting in a more flexible manner. The new equipment and doctrines were tested at a new Marine facility, 29 Palms in southern California, where Marine units scheduled to deploy conducted realistic, life fire combined-arms training exercises in the desert. The Corps' new emphasis on defending Norway in the event of the Cold War turning hot led to increased use of another training facility in the Sierra Nevada Mountains at Bridgeport, California. At these two installations Marines trained, providentially, in precisely the sort of environments they would fight in at the start of the 21st century.

In the late 20th century it became increasingly difficult for the Marine Corps to live up to the World War I recruiting poster slogan "First to Fight." Modern aircraft and mid-air refueling techniques enabled light infantry forces to deploy with unheard of speed anywhere in the world where friendly airstrips awaited them. The first land-based aerial unit was the 1st Tactical Fighter Wing of the U.S. Air Force, which deployed from Langley, Virginia on August 8, 1990. On August 9 they began conducting combat air patrols. The first American ground troops to arrive in Saudi Arabia were the men of the 2d Brigade, 82d Airborne Division; this was the duty "ready" brigade of the division. They began deploying to Saudi Arabia by air beginning August 8 and the brigade was fully deployed on August 14. The rest of the 82d Airborne Division was fully deployed to Saudi Arabia on August 24. In addition, carrier task forces built around the USS *Dwight D. Eisenhower* (CVN 69) and USS *Independence* (CV 62) were within strike range.

These formidable forces might not have been able to stop a determined Iraqi-armored assault into Saudi Arabia, however;

the 82d Airborne's brigades were light infantry units with little in the way of supporting arms and its mission was initially limited to defending the Saudi airfields and acting as a "trip-wire" force should Iraq invade the Desert Kingdom. The Marines were not the first forces to deploy to Saudi Arabia, but their deployment provided the muscle needed to make Operation *Desert Shield* a reality. Moving combat power rapidly ashore has long been a Marine capability, but in the Gulf War Marine power was not projected by amphibious assault, instead it was projected through a new program, Maritime Prepositioning.

The Maritime Prepositioning program was a response to a perceived weakness in America's strategic posture; the Iran Hostage crisis put a spotlight on America's inability to project power into the Persian Gulf region, despite the region's relative importance. In Europe and the Pacific the United States maintained large bases on the territory of allies but this was neither practical nor feasible in the Middle East. The program put all of the equipment for a Marine expeditionary brigade as well as enough supplies for the brigade to fight for 30 days on a squadron of purpose-built vessels of the U.S. Military Sea Lift Command. The personnel and personal equipment of the brigade would be deployed by the Military Airlift Command to the region where it could rendezvous with a Maritime Prepositioning Squadron. The concept required a friendly host nation with well-developed airfields and ports, and in the 1980s a great deal of aid was given to the various Gulf States and Saudi Arabia to build up the infrastructure required to support a rapid military deployment in the region if required.

Maritime Prepositioning Ships are civilian-crewed vessels with a squadron staff of U.S. Navy. In 1990, Maritime Prepositioning Squadron One served the Mediterranean, Squadron Three served the western Pacific, and Squadron Two was based at Diego Garcia and covered the Indian Ocean and Middle East. Squadrons Two and Three deployed in support of Operation *Desert Shield*, with Squadron Two deploying from Diego Garcia on August 8.

Marines of the 7th Marine Expeditionary Brigade, commanded by Major General John I. Hopkins, arrived in Saudi Arabia mid-August, where they joined with the equipment from Maritime Prepositioning Squadron Two. The 7th Marine Expeditionary Brigade, like all Marine Air-Ground task forces, was a tripartite formation, with a ground, air, and logistics component.

As Lieutenant General Joseph P. Hoar later noted in a lecture he gave at the Marine Corps Historical Center in April, 1991:

> The 7th Marine Expeditionary Brigade was the first ground element that had tanks and armored personnel carriers. It was the first element that was capable of meeting the threat that existed in Kuwait. But it was more than that; it was an air-ground team as we all know, that had fixed wing, rotary wing ... had an air-ground task force headquarters. It had its full suite of logistics for 30 days, so it was self-sustaining for 30 days. ...Marine forces were arriving not only with that combat power, ready to be put into operation, but in addition to that brought its logistics as well.

While military forces were deploying in Saudi Arabia proper to defend against a possible Iraqi invasion, amphibious assault forces also arrived. The 13th Marine Expeditionary Unit (Special Operations Capable) and the 4th Marine Expeditionary Brigade, commanded by Major General Harry W. Jenkins, Jr., had both arrived in the Persian Gulf by mid-September and formed the landing forces for an Amphibious Task Force. The Marine expeditionary forces in the Amphibious Task Force were intended as a theater reserve, and their employment was controlled directly by General Schwartzkopf. During *Desert Shield*, they were prepared to reinforce the troops defending Saudi Arabia if needed, or to launch amphibious assaults or raids against the enemy's rear if the Iraqis attacked Saudi Arabia. Their presence was also intended to divert Iraqi forces towards defending the coast, reducing the number of troops faced ashore.

During the Gulf War the Marine Corps were equipped almost as an armored division. An M60A1 of Task Force Papa Bear, part of the 1st Marine Division, sits before a burning oil well during the liberation of Kuwait. The armored Marines performed extremely well, fighting off several Iraqi armored attacks while suffer few losses. This photograph was taken at approximately 1500. In an attempt to slow the American offensive, the Iraqis had set fire to Kuwait's oil wells. (Official USMC photograph)

In support of this, Operation *Imminent Thunder* was conducted from November 15–21, 1990. This training exercise was intended to test the plan for defending Saudi Arabia and determine what issues would arise from the large "joint/combined"* forces working together in the Desert Kingdom. The exercise amphibious landings were originally planned for Ras al-Mishab, but the proximity to the Kuwaiti border and possibility of unintentional conflict with Iraqi forces led to

---

* In American military parlance, "joint" operations are conducted by multiple services (Navy-Army, Air Force-Marine Corps, etc.) while "combined" operations are conducted by American forces in conjunction with allied foreign military forces. Operation *Desert Shield*, conducted by forces from all U.S. armed services as well as the military forces of several other nations including among others Saudi Arabia, Great Britain, France, etc., was a "joint/combined" operation.

General Schwarzkopf shifting the exercise south, to Ras al-Ghar. The new site was much more accessible to the media, which was eager for any new footage as the confrontation continued into its third month. Marine amphibious capabilities received a great deal of press attention as a result, and the Amphibious Task Force commander, Rear Admiral John B. LaPlante, later described it as "beating our chest for the press." Ironically, much of the amphibious landing was canceled due to dangerous seas, but the extensive air and communication exercises were a success.

In January, 1991, as the coalition worked to build forces for the liberation of Kuwait, the U.S. Navy and Marine Corps demonstrated the flexibility and versatility of naval forces by undertaking Operation *Eastern Exit*, the evacuation of the U.S. embassy in Mogadishu, Somalia. The ongoing Somalian civil war created an unsafe situation in the capital of Mogadishu as order crumbled and various militias began fighting openly throughout the city. The U.S. ambassador's request to evacuate the embassy was approved on January 2, 1991.

In January 1991, the U.S. Navy and Marine Corps demonstrated the flexibility and versatility of naval forces by undertaking Operation *Eastern Exit*—the evacuation of the U.S. embassy in Mogadishu, Somalia—in the midst of the preparations for Operation *Desert Storm* during the Gulf War. The Navy and Marine amphibious forces in the Persian Gulf, who were preparing to help liberate Kuwait, were given this task.

Colonel James Doyle Jr., commanding officer of Brigade Service Support Group 4, was appointed the Marine commander of the evacuation, and Captain Alan B. Moser, USN, commander of Amphibious Squadron 6, was appointed commander of the amphibious task force. Both the USS *Guam* and USS *Trenton* sailed immediately south with elements of the 4th Marine Expeditionary Brigade on board to conduct the evacuation.

Three Marines climb the side of a berm as they move forward into attack positions during Operation Desert Storm. *Although the Iraqis attempted to counterattack with armored forces, their defenses had to be breached by Marine infantry before the tanks could move in. The Iraqis had a constructed a classic defense in depth position in Kuwait. (Official USMC photograph)*

On January 4, the U.S. ambassador reported the embassy was under siege by looters, and that night Marine helicopters flew 450 miles (being refueled twice en route by Marine C-130s) and landed a security detail of Navy SEALS and Marines from Company C, 1st Battalion, 2d Marines. They evacuated 61 civilians and returned to the amphibious task force. The next night, while the Marines provided perimeter security, the helicopters evacuated over 200 more civilians. By the morning of January 6, 1991, less than four days after receiving the order, the evacuation was complete. Two hundred and eighty-one civilians from 31 countries, including Great Britain, Germany, Kenya, Kuwait, Nigeria, Oman, the Soviet Union, Sudan, Turkey, and the United Arab Emirates, were evacuated (the wife of the Nigerian ambassador gave birth on board the USS

From the beginning, Marine Air has prided itself on its ability to operate from expeditionary airfields. These two Marine AH-1 Cobra helicopters on the ground are being refueled during Operation Restore Hope *in Somalia. (Official USMC photograph)*

Guam en route to Oman, increasing the number of evacuees to 282).

Thanking the sailors and Marines for the swift, efficient evacuation, the U.S. ambassador said, "Few of us would have been alive today if we had been outside your reach.... We will take a part of each of you with us for the rest of our lives." The Navy and Marines forces involved immediately returned to operations in the Gulf.

When the Allied air attacks against Iraq began on January 17, 1991, the sea-borne feint needed reinforcement in order to remain credible. Amphibious raids were one method of reinforcing that threat. On January 23, 1991, Captain Thomas L. McClelland, USN, commanding Amphibious Squadron 5, and Colonel John E. Rhodes, commander of the 13th Marine Expeditionary Unit (Special Operations *Capable*) were ordered to plan for an amphibious raid on several Iraqi-held Kuwaiti islands, code-named Operation *Desert Sting*. Iraqis on one of the targeted islands, Qurah, surrendered on January 25 to the USS *Curtis* (FFG 38). On January 26 the Iraqis' garrison on

Although there has been little need since World War II, Marine amphibious capabilities provide the Corps with strategic mobility and operational versatility. Two Marine armored amphibious vehicles from the 15th Marine Expeditionary Unit emerge from the surf onto the beach at Mogadishu Airport, Somalia, as part of Operation Restore Hope. *(Official USMC photograph)*

another of the targeted islands, Umm al Maradim, created a sign indicating they wished to surrender to U.S. Navy reconnaissance aircraft that photographed the island. The plan for Operation *Desert Sting* was modified accordingly.

Heavily supported by Navy aircraft, Company A, Battalion Landing Team 1/4 (Reinforced) landed on the north end of Maradim Island at noon on January 29. They encountered no enemy fire or other resistance and found the island had been deserted by its garrison. The Marines captured or destroyed a large quantity of small arms, machine guns and mortars, as well as several Iraqi anti-aircraft guns and missiles. After three hours on the island the raid force departed, leaving a Kuwaiti flag raised over the island and the words "Free Kuwait" and "USMC" on several of the buildings.

After the decision to liberate Kuwait was made in November, the question of an amphibious landing in Kuwait remained open until February 2 at a conference on the USS *Blue Ridge* (LCC-19) between General Schwarzkopf, the Navy theater commander, Vice Admiral Stanley R. Arthur, and the Marine theater commander, General Walter Boomer, concerning amphibious operations. At the conference, it was clear the Navy was not ready to conduct any large amphibious operations, in large part because of the number of mines the Iraqis had deployed to Kuwaiti waters. General Schwarzkopf was not enthusiastic either, since he was informed during the meeting that the amphibious operation and subsequent coastal fighting would probably involve massive destruction to Kuwait's most densely populated areas. He remarked that he was "not going to destroy Kuwait in order to save it." Asked if he required the landing, General Boomer said no, with the caveat that the amphibious deception and mine clearing continue, and that the amphibious forces continue planning so the option would remain if it was needed.

Although General Schwarzkopf had vetoed a major amphibious invasion, an amphibious feint remained an important part of the coalition's plan, in order to draw attention away from both the Marine thrust into central Kuwait and the Army's wide, sweeping flanking movement to the west. The American battleships conducted naval gunfire support missions along the coast throughout February, and coalition minelayers began clearing lanes through the Iraqi minefields.

The U.S. Navy's fear of Iraqi mines and lack of confidence in its ability to fully clear the mine fields proved well-founded. On February 17 USS *Tripoli* (LPH 10) was disabled after it hit a mine. *Tripoli* had been pressed into service as the platform for the Sikorsky MH-53E Sea Dragon helicopters of the Navy's Mine Countermeasures Helicopter Squadron 14 during minesweeping operations and was ironically engaged in this service when it struck a mine. Later the same day USS *Princeton* (CG 59) was also struck by a mine. Fortunately, neither vessel suffered fatalities from the mine attacks.

After the war, the commander of the Iraqi Navy declared that, "these [Iraqi] mines proved [their] lethality and effectiveness … they caused havoc within the enemy force. …During the epic Mother of All Battles, this weapon [mines] was utilized effectively and successfully to disrupt the allies' plans in launching any operation from the sea." His view was shared by the U.S. Navy Central Command commander, Vice-Admiral Stanley R. Arthur, who later stated, "Iraq successfully delayed and might have prevented an amphibious assault on Kuwait's assailable flank, protected a large part of its force from the effects of naval gunfire, and severely hampered surface operations in the northern Arabian Gulf, all through the use of naval mines."

It was clear the Iraqis took the amphibious threat seriously. In November, Iraq's General Military Intelligence Directorate (GMID) sent a series of reports to the Iraqi military forces in the Kuwaiti theater, detailing expected Coalition invasion routes and operational intentions. The report showed that the Iraqis were keenly aware of American amphibious capabilities: "The enemy will conduct naval landing operations simultaneously with land and air operations to isolate as many troops as possible and support land operations from the sea with heavy artillery fire."

The successful liberation provided further examples of the Iraqi reaction to the amphibious feint, as the Kuwaiti coast was peppered with Iraqi beach defenses and fighting positions. One of the more interesting finds was in a school near the embassy. In the gymnasium the Iraqis had constructed a large sand table detailing the defenses they had placed around Kuwait City, complete with toy artillery pieces, Lego blocks, and small signs identifying Iraqi units. The sand table was very clear evidence of the success of the amphibious deception in diverting Iraqi forces to the coast. Major General James M. Myatt, commander of the 1st Marine Division, recalled, "I think what we can't dismiss is the level of effort put into the defenses along the beaches by the Iraqis … probably 40% to 50% of the Iraqi artillery pieces were pointed to the east in defense of this perceived real threat—an attack from the Gulf. There were literally hundreds of antiaircraft weapon systems laid in a direct-fire mode from Saudi Arabia all the way up way above Kuwait City to defend against the amphibious threat … I think it saved a lot of Marine lives."

At the beginning of the 21st century the Corps was better equipped, educated, and trained, riding high on the operational and tactical successes of the Gulf War. Taking inspiration from early Marine thinkers Lieutenant Colonel Earl H. "Pete" Ellis and Major General Smedley D. Butler, visionary Commandant General Alfred M. Gray Jr. created Marine Corps University at Quantico in 1989 as a center for military excellence and education. He also ordered the publication of *Warfighting* (FMFM-1), creating a doctrinal publication that immediately joined the *Small Wars Manual* (1940) and *Advanced Base Operations in Micronesia* (1921) as the "Holy Trinity" of legendary Marine doctrinal works.

General Anthony C. Zinni was born in 1943, and was commissioned a second lieutenant in the Marine Corps in 1965. He served two tours in Vietnam, as an advisor to the Vietnamese Marine Corps in 1967, and as a company commander with 1st Battalion, 5th Marines. In between those tours he served as an instructor at The Basic School. He was wounded in Vietnam during his 1970 tour, and was awarded the Purple Heart.

In the 1970s and 1980s he commanded the 2d Battalion, 8th Marines, the 9th Marines, and the 35th Marine Expeditionary Unit. In 1991 he served as the Chief of Staff and Deputy Commanding General of Combined Task Force Provide Comfort during the Kurdish relief effort in Turkey and Iraq.

In 1992, General Zinni was serving as Director of Operations for Unified Task Force Somalia. In that capacity he often met with Mohamed Farrah Aideed, then the leading Somali warlord; for these visits his driver, a Corporal Watts, would organize a squad from the headquarters staff for security. In *Battle Ready* (2004), General Zinni described one memorable meeting with Aideed:

> I was greeted by shocked faces on Aideed's men. I turned to the second Humvee in line, which seemed to be the source of all the excitement: An African American woman Marine was

standing there in her battle gear, with her M-16 at the ready, looking tough as hell.

I left to conduct my business. Forty-five minutes later, when I came back out, the stir was still at high pitch. It was obvious the Somalis couldn't believe their eyes—an armed woman in Marine battle dress.

On the way back, I turned to Corporal Watts. "You brought a woman Marine, huh," I said; I knew he'd set this scene up.

He smiled. "She'll kill you just as dead as any man," he said.

I laughed. He loved jerking the Somali tough guys' chains. Back to our headquarters, I drew the woman Marine aside for a quick chat. Corporal Watts was right. She'd kill you just as dead as any man could.

From 1994 to 1996, Zinni served as the commanding general of I Marine Expeditionary Force. During this period General Zinni served as commander of the Combined Task Force for Operation *United Shield*, protecting the withdrawal of U.N. forces from Somalia. He took command of United States Central Command in 1997; he oversaw Operation *Desert Fox*, the 1998 airstrikes against Iraq. In 2000 he retired from the Marine Corps. In 2004, Zinni poignantly wrote:

> Moral courage is often more difficult than physical courage. There are times when you disagree and you have to suck it in and say, "Yes, sir," and go do what you're told. There are also times when you disagree and you have to speak out, even at the cost of your career. If you're a general, you might have to throw your stars on the table, as they say, and resign for the sake of some principle or truth from which you can't back away.

The attack of 9/11 initiated the Global War on Terrorism; a series of conflicts varying in intensity from the massive conventional invasion of Iraq in 2003 to advise-and-assist missions across the globe. Serving alongside the U.S. Army in counterinsurgency campaigns in Afghanistan and Iraq, the Marine Corps faced a myriad and ever-changing roster of evolving foes alongside the other services in an increasingly joint operational environment.

Throughout these conflicts, the senior leadership of the Marine Corps thrived. Five Marine generals have commanded U.S. Central Command (the most active theater of the last three decades) from when it was founded in 1983 to 2019. One of those Marines, General James N. Mattis became secretary of defense in 2017. For the first time since the Joint Staff was created, two Marines served as chairman of the Joint Chiefs of Staff, General Peter Pace (2005–7) and General Joseph F. Dunford Jr. (2015–present). The Marine Corps' influence on the making of grand strategy of the United States has never been greater.

On November 26, 2001, 1st Battalion, 1st Marines raised the flag over Forward Operating Base Rhino, near the city of Kandahar in southern Afghanistan. This was one of the first FOBs established in Afghanistan; the air strip had been raided by 3d Ranger Battalion, 75th Ranger Regiment in October, and then, in late November, the 15th Marine Expeditionary Force had launched itself 400 miles from the sea to establish a forward base there. On December 17, 2001 the U.S. embassy was reopened by the State Department and the security force from the 26th Marine Expeditionary Unit (26th MEU) performed the ceremonial flag raising. During Operation *Anaconda* in southern Afghanistan, Marine Cobra helicopter gunships flew in support of the 10th Mountain and 101st Airmobile division troops fighting in the mountains.

The Global War on Terror was waged in the shadows with advisors and support provided to regimes endangered by terrorist movements, but another large scale conflict with Iraq came in 2003.

Marines marched on Baghdad intent on demonstrating that the war was against Saddam Hussein and his government, not the people of Iraq. Major General James N. Mattis reminded his troops of earlier orders forbidding displays of triumphalism and displays of the American flag. The 1st Marine Division's unit history later stated, "The Marines complied with the order, not without some mixed emotions. ...Very soon, the Marines would come to take great pride in their actions as liberators, and of the actions of their own Nation. What other country would act like this in victory? The Marines did not need flags to display their fierce pride, it was present in the faces that peered out from under their dusty helmets."

The Marines found their moment on April 9 as they advanced into Baghdad. Marines of 3d Battalion, 4th Marines were ordered to secure buildings in the center of downtown Baghdad. They encountered less resistance than expected and met a large crowd of Iraqis at the Firdos Square traffic circle. Journalists who had been confined under Saddam's regime to the nearby hotels were reporting on the large crowds and the Marines. At the center of Firdos Square there was a large statue of Saddam Hussein. The Marines and Iraqis started working together to bring the statue down and an M88 Recovery Vehicle from the 1st Tank Battalion was brought forward. One of the recovery vehicles' crewmen, Corporal Edward Chin, of Company B, 1st Tank Battalion climbed the derrick and draped an American flag over the statue's head. The Iraqis called for an Iraqi flag instead, and one was quickly produced from the crowd. The Marines replaced the American flag with the Iraqi flag, and then proceeded to topple the statue. Later, some of the Iraqi participants would express regret for the toppling, preferring in retrospect the tyranny of Saddam to the years of bloodshed and anarchy that followed. But on that April morning, the Marines and the Iraqi civilians had acted together to topple the dictator's symbol, and raise the symbol of the Iraqi people.

Unfortunately, such cooperation with the Iraqis broke down in the wake of the liberation of Iraq, and a counterinsurgency soon sprang up there, fueled by internal Iraqi sectarian differences, American ignorance of local conditions, and opportunistic foreign terrorist fighters who flocked to Iraq hoping to cause an American defeat similar to that suffered in Vietnam or Somalia.

After being withdrawn from Iraq in 2003, the Marines returned to fight primarily in the Anbar province of western Iraq. These forces represented the Marine Corps' commitment in 2004 to its "Expeditionary Maneuver Warfare" concept which emphasized "strategically agile and tactically flexible Marine Air-Ground Task Forces (MAGTFs) with the operational reach to project power directly against critical points in the littorals and beyond." Although the Marine Corps had an extensive history with counterinsurgency (COIN) warfare, in 2004 the doctrinal focus remained on the ideas of maneuver warfare, which utilized "high-tempo operations and surprise with a bias for action to achieve operational advantage—physical, temporal, and conditional—over an enemy. The aim is to defeat the enemy by shattering his cohesion and to prevail by rapidly responding to events, if not anticipating them before they occur." In 2004, in both Iraq and Afghanistan, the challenge was to adapt this maneuver warfare mindset to the COIN environment which then dominated Iraq and Afghanistan.

In 2004 the insurgency in Iraq was increasing in ferocity, much of the attention of Central Command and the Marine Corps was focused on Operation *Iraqi Freedom*. The I Marine Expeditionary Force returned to Iraq and took over control of Iraq's volatile al-Anbar province. Its deployment would culminate in the battle of Fallujah by the end of 2004.

Marine tactics evolved, as they conducted large clearing operations aimed at pacification in Iraqi cities while partnering with local tribes to deny the terrorists safe havens. In late 2004, these tactics led to the clearance of the city of Fallujah during Operation *Phantom Fury*. In the largest urban battle for the Marine Corps since the battle for Hue City during the Vietnam War, Marine, Army, and Iraqi battalions fought for Fallujah from November 7, 2004 through December 24, 2004.

Only one Marine so far has been awarded the Medal of Honor for the fighting in Iraq. Corporal Jason L. Dunham was serving

Sergeant Jeff Seabaugh, squad leader with the 15th Marine Expeditionary Unit (Special Operations Capable), moves his Marines in Zubayr, Iraq, on March 23, 2003 during Operation Iraqi Freedom. The war in Iraq forced the Marines into a familiar role, training indigenous military forces while conducting a counterinsurgency campaign. (Official USMC photograph)

as a squad leader with Kilo Company, 3rd Battalion, 7th Marines on April 14, 2004, when he was awarded the Medal of Honor:

Corporal Dunham's squad was conducting a reconnaissance mission in the town of Karabilah, Iraq, when they heard rocket-propelled grenade and small arms fire erupt approximately two kilometers to the west. Corporal Dunham led his Combined Anti-Armor Team towards the engagement to provide fire support to their Battalion Commander's convoy, which had been ambushed as it was traveling to Camp Husaybah. As Corporal Dunham and his Marines advanced, they quickly began to receive enemy fire. Corporal Dunham ordered his squad to dismount their vehicles and led one of his fire teams on foot several blocks south of the ambushed convoy. Discovering seven Iraqi vehicles in a column attempting to depart, Corporal Dunham and his team stopped the vehicles to search them for weapons. As they approached the vehicles, an insurgent leaped out and attacked Corporal Dunham. Corporal Dunham wrestled the insurgent to the ground and in the ensuing struggle saw the insurgent release a grenade. Corporal Dunham immediately alerted his fellow Marines to the threat. Aware of the imminent danger and without hesitation, Corporal Dunham covered the grenade with his helmet and body, bearing the brunt of the explosion and shielding his Marines from the blast. In an ultimate and selfless act of bravery in which he was mortally wounded, he saved the lives of at least two fellow Marines.

Marine counterinsurgency strategy continued to bear fruit, resulting in the "Anbar Awakening" which gave the Iraqis, at

Lance Corporal Brandy L. Guerrero, radio operator, Communications Detachment, MEU Service Support Group 11, 11th Marine Expeditionary Unit (Special Operations Capable), kisses an Iraqi baby waiting to be examined during a humanitarian assistance operation in the village of ash-Shafiyah, Iraq. This operation provided medical and dental treatments to Iraqis during Operation Iraqi Freedom. Marines provided medical care and other support to Iraqi civilians during the Iraq war. (Official USMC photograph)

least temporarily, control of the province. After the successful campaign, Marine forces were withdrawn from Iraq in 2008.

In February 2004, the 22d Marine Expeditionary Unit (Special Operations Capable) (22d MEU), boarded the amphibious warfare ships of Expeditionary Strike Group 2 and proceeded across the Atlantic towards the seas of the Middle East via the Mediterranean. Expeditionary Strike Group 2 was built around the amphibious assault ship USS *Wasp* (LHD 1), amphibious transport dock USS *Shreveport* (LPD 12), and dock landing ship USS *Whidbey Island* (LSD 41). The 22d Marine Expeditionary Unit (Special Operations Capable) provided the landing force and airpower for the amphibious task force, and the naval punch was provided by the cruisers USS *Yorktown* (CG 48) and USS *Leyte Gulf* (CG 55), the destroyer USS *McFaul* (DDG 74), and attack submarine USS *Connecticut* (SSN 22). This amphibious task force represented U.S. Central Command's strategic reserve as it directed Operation *Enduring Freedom* in Afghanistan, Operation *Iraqi Freedom* in Iraq, and ongoing operations for the War on Terror elsewhere within its area of responsibility.

In 2004, Afghanistan was struggling to establish its first real government after decades of war and chaos. In December 2001 the Bonn Agreement set the plan for the new government. The first national elections were originally scheduled for July of 2004, but were delayed until October due to security concerns caused by a Taleban resurgence.

American military forces in Afghanistan were commanded by Combined Forces Command-Afghanistan led in 2004 by Lieutenant General David W. Barno, USA. Under Barno, American military operations in Afghanistan were divided between operating forces under Combined Joint Task Force 180 (CJTF-180)[*] and training forces under the Office of Military Cooperation-Afghanistan. General Barno shifted the focus of the American military effort in Afghanistan from destruction

---

[*] CJTF-180 was built around the headquarters of the 10th Mountain Division at the beginning of 2004.

of enemy forces to a counterinsurgency approach focusing on the people of Afghanistan. The Taleban challenge to the 2004 elections was a direct threat to this population-focused strategy, and CJTF-180 planned Operation *Mountain Storm* in order to provide the security environment the elections required.

Central Command ordered 22d Marine Expeditionary Unit to serve as the main effort of Operation *Mountain Storm*, in order to preempt the spring Taleban offensive and stabilize Afghanistan enough to allow the national elections to occur. Operation *Mountain Storm* called for the Marines to cross Afghanistan to the airfield at Kandahar, and then proceed to Uruzgan province where they would create an environment that would allow for unmolested voter registration and later, elections.

Uruzgan province is one of Afghanistan's central provinces. It is predominantly Pashtun, extremely rural and mountainous. The mujahedeen of Uruzgan were among the first to join the Taleban when it was founded it in the 1990s. The province was underdeveloped and rugged, accessible from Kandahar by only two mountain passes. Uruzgan was long considered a Taleban stronghold, its geography and culture suiting it well to the methods of guerrilla warfare and insurgency.

Commanded by Colonel Kenneth F. McKenzie Jr., the 22d Marine Expeditionary Unit's major subordinate commands were Battalion Landing Team, 1st Battalion, 6th Marines (BLT 1/6) commanded by Lieutenant Colonel Asad A. Khan, Marine Medium Helicopter Squadron 266 (Reinforced) (HMH-266) commanded by Lieutenant Colonel Joel R. Powers, and MEU Service Support Group 22 (MSSG-22) commanded by Lieutenant Colonel Benjamin R. Braden.

Colonel McKenzie's staff thoroughly coordinated and planned the operation with CJTF-180 and were prepared to conduct "combat operations to defeat anti-Coalition militants (ACMs), secure major population areas, and support civil military operations (CMO) in AO Linebacker [Uruzgan] to create a secure and stable environment in order to facilitate United Nations Assistance Mission in Afghanistan (UNAMA)-sponsored voter registration and elections." Early in the planning stages for Operation *Mountain Storm*, CJTF-180 made two decisions that Colonel McKenzie later identified as key to the success of the mission. The Marine Expeditionary Unit was assigned its own area of operations for Uruzgan province, which gave Colonel McKenzie freedom of movement. Second, the force was employed as a fully functioning Marine Air-Ground Task Force rather than being cannibalized and split up amongst American and allied forces in Afghanistan.

Colonel McKenzie's staff created a four-phase plan for Operation *Mountain Storm*. In Phase I they would shape the battlefield, opening contact with civilians in the region, reconnoitering, and choosing the site required for the forward operating base. In Phase II the "bowl" around Tarin Kowt would be secured and the forward operating base established. In Phase III southern Uruzgan would be secured and voter registration would begin. In Phase IV, the final phase, operations would be conducted against Taleban sanctuaries in northern Uruzgan, securing the province and enabling a successful election.

In late March, after the 420-mile transit across Pakistan to Kandahar from the amphibious warships of Expeditionary Strike Group 2, the 22d Marine Expeditionary Unit began Phase I of Operation *Mountain Storm*, shaping and preparing the battlefield. Five long-range patrols were conducted into the province, with the Marines surveying the ground, selecting a site for the required forward operating base, and liaising with U.S. Army Special Forces teams in the area. Colonel McKenzie spent two days coordinating with Governor Jan Mohammad Khan in Tarin Kowet. A Marine liaison officer from Colonel McKenzie's staff was attached to the governor's staff, providing secure communications with the Afghan civilian authority. The Marines saw first contact with the enemy when one of the patrols moving through the mountain pass was struck by an improvised explosive device, destroying a vehicle and seriously wounding a Marine. This was the only effective IED attack on the 22d MEU during this deployment.

Knowing that subsequent operations would involve searching Afghan females, and that this could breed resentment among the locals if male Marines conducted these searches against Afghan custom, Colonel McKenzie ordered the formation of female search teams to deploy with the infantry. Initially, three female sailors and nine female marines were selected and divided into two teams of six. Each team was attached to an infantry company through the later phases of Operation *Mountain Storm*. The teams searched Afghan civilians throughout the operation, and though under fire several times they suffered no casualties.

On April 25, McKenzie's command began Phase II of the operation. Three rifle companies of 1st Battalion, 6th Marines conducted air assaults into Taleban-controlled areas of the province, capturing caches of weapons and pushing the Taleban onto the defensive as six large convoys carried the equipment and supplies of Lieutenant Colonel Braden's logistics units to the dirt airfield just outside Tarin Kowt that was chosen for Forward Operating Base Ripley.* Ripley featured a 6,000-foot runway, a complete helicopter fueling and rearming point, and 13 helicopter landing pads.

Phase III of Operation *Mountain Storm* kicked off on May 11, after Forward Operating Base Ripley was fully functional. The Marines began to work with Governor Khan's provincial government and the United Nations voter registration teams to get voters registered in the province. Area security was provided to voter registration sites (prior to the arrival of the marines, it was considered to unsafe to for these teams to operate in Uruzgan) and civil affairs projects were begun in order to establish the new Afghanistan government as a superior option to the Taleban. During this phase combat action was light, as the Taleban generally choose to retire rather than engage the Marines. Company-sized patrol actions failed to bring the enemy to battle as they swept through the southern part of the province.

---

* The FOB was named after Marine Colonel John W. Ripley, who earned the Navy Cross at the bridge of Dong Ha during the Vietnam War.

The Marines determined that the Taleban's centers of resistance were in the highlands surrounding Tarin Kowt, especially Dey Chopan to the east and Cehar Cineh to the west.

Operation *Asbury Park* launched on June 1, opening Phase IV of the 22d Marine Expeditionary Unit's plan to secure Uruzgan province. Operating a large patrol commanded by Lieutenant Colonel Khan and mounted entirely in HMMWVs and locally purchased vehicles, and reinforced with Afghanistan militia led by Governor Khan, the Marines scoured the Dey Chopan highlands. The Marines of 1st Battalion, 6th Marines fought eight engagements, employing all of their weapons and calling in numerous airstrikes from the plethora of available air support, killing scores of Taleban while suffering only 14 wounded in return.

The success of Operation *Asbury Park* convinced CJTF-76* to extend 22d Marine Expeditionary Unit's tour in Afghanistan and reinforce their success by placing the 2d Battalion, 5th Infantry (2/5) of the Army's 25th Infantry Division (Light) under Colonel McKenzie's tactical control. With two infantry battalions available, Operations *Thunder Bolt* and *Asbury Park II* were planned to simultaneously strike the Cehar Cineh and Dey Chopan highlands respectively.

Both operations uncovered numerous caches of weapons, but the Taleban's strategy returned to avoidance and disengagement. They chose to retire from Uruzgan province or faded back into the civilian population. In July, with Uruzgan province seemingly pacified, 22d Marine Expeditionary Unit exfiltrated back through Pakistan to waiting ships of Expeditionary Strike Group 2.

The deployment of the Marines to Uruzgan greatly aided the United Nation's voter registration drive, and reduced Taleban attacks in the province to nearly zero in the short term. Locals were cooperating with troops, and even leading them to IED and

---

* CJTF-180 changed in mid-April 2004 to the 25th Infantry Division (Light), resulting in a designator change to CJTF-76.

weapons caches in 2005. The Taleban gradually became more assertive in the province and an American soldier and Afghan soldier were killed there later in 2005.

The NATO-led International Security Assistance Force (ISAF) gradually took over control of security in much of Afghanistan, and in 2006 the Dutch forces of the ISAF became the lead force in Uruzgan province. The Dutch pressured President Karzai to remove Governor Jan Mohammad Kahn in 2006 due to his ties to the drug trade. He became an advisor to President Karzai and continued to build his influence until he was assassinated in 2011.

It was estimated that in 2006 98% of insurgents in Uruzgan were originally from Uruzgan, suggesting that there was significant Taleban influence/disapproval of the government and that the Taleban were still effectively recruiting. The Dutch approach was to establish contact with the civilian population and focus on supporting the local government rather than combat patrols aimed at killing insurgents. The Dutch left the province in 2010 when internal Dutch politics lead to their withdrawal.

In July 2012 the Afghan National Army and Afghan National Police began to take over security for the province and coalition forces began to pull out after an announcement by Karzai in April that Afghan forces were ready to take over the job.

22d Marine Expeditionary Unit's operations in Uruzgan province highlighted the strategic and operational flexibility of the MAGTF, even in counterinsurgency operations, but also revealed the limitations of the concept. Colonel McKenzie's 2,400 sailors and Marines secured the province and dramatically, albeit temporarily, reduced Taleban attacks in the region. The initial effort was not reinforced when the MAGTF withdrew, and the Taleban was able to continue to influence, recruit, and maneuver in the province.

Corporal Dakota L. Meyer was awarded the Medal of Honor for risking his life above and beyond the call of duty while serving while serving with Marine Embedded Training Team

2-8, Regional Corps Advisory Command 3-7, in Kunar province, Afghanistan, on September 8, 2009. The citation reads:

Corporal Meyer maintained security at a patrol rally point while other members of his team moved on foot with two platoons of Afghan National Army and Border Police into the village of Ganjgal for a pre-dawn meeting with village elders. Moving into the village, the patrol was ambushed by more than 50 enemy fighters firing rocket propelled grenades, mortars, and machine guns from houses and fortified positions on the slopes above. Hearing over the radio that four U.S. team members were cut off, Corporal Meyer seized the initiative. With a fellow Marine driving, Corporal Meyer took the exposed gunner's position in a gun-truck as they drove down the steeply terraced terrain in a daring attempt to disrupt the enemy attack and locate the trapped U.S. team. Disregarding intense enemy fire now concentrated on their lone vehicle, Corporal Meyer killed a number of enemy fighters with the mounted machine guns and his rifle, some at near point blank range, as he and his driver made three solo trips into the ambush area. During the first two trips, he and his driver evacuated two dozen Afghan soldiers, many of whom were wounded. When one machine gun became inoperable, he directed a return to the rally point to switch to another gun-truck for a third trip into the ambush area where his accurate fire directly supported the remaining U.S. personnel and Afghan soldiers fighting their way out of the ambush. Despite a shrapnel wound to his arm, Corporal Meyer made two more trips into the ambush area in a third gun-truck accompanied by four other Afghan vehicles to recover more wounded Afghan soldiers and search for the missing U.S. team members. Still under heavy enemy fire, he dismounted the vehicle on the fifth trip and moved on foot to locate and recover the bodies of his team members. Meyer's daring initiative and bold fighting spirit throughout the 6-hour battle significantly disrupted the enemy's attack and inspired the members of the combined force to fight on.

U.S. Marines with India Company, 3rd Battalion, 5th Marine Regiment provide covering fire for fellow Marines as they move out of a danger area after taking sniper fire during a security patrol in Sangin, Afghanistan, on November 2, 2010. The Marines found themselves fighting a classic counterinsurgency in Afghanistan, going from providing medical care to impoverished locals to a fire fight with guerrillas to meeting with local leaders to discuss building a school within a few hours. (Official USMC photograph)

In late 2009, President Barack H. Obama determined that the situation in Afghanistan required a surge of troop reinforcements. For the U.S. Marine Corps, this meant that the Marine involvement in that theater of the Global War on Terrorism would continue to intensify. A Marine expeditionary brigade was deployed to Afghanistan in 2009, where the troop surge and increased Marine presence led to the Marines taking control of security operations for Helmand and Nimroz provinces in 2010. The Corps' insistence on autonomy within its provinces led to the nickname "Marineistan."

The Marine Corps approached its increased role in Afghanistan with enthusiasm, employing the Corps' traditional expertise in counterinsurgency (COIN) warfare acquired through the Banana Wars and the Vietnam War as well as lessons learned more recently in Iraq during the al-Anbar Awakening. Along with this focus on the application of COIN doctrine, the Marine Corps fielded the Bell Boeing MV-22 Osprey tiltrotor military aircraft, fully replacing the venerable Boeing Vertol CH-46 Sea Knight helicopters that had been the Corps' primary medium-lift airframe for troops and cargo. Additionally, the recently created U.S. Marine Corps Forces Special Operations Command (MARSOC) fully participated in U.S. Special Operations Command's Afghanistan missions during this period.

———————

The presidential unit citation to the **Marine Expeditionary Brigade-Afghanistan** for their outstanding performance in action against enemy forces from May 29, 2009 to April 12, 2010, in support of Operation *Enduring Freedom*:

> Marine Expeditionary Brigade-Afghanistan conducted the most holistic counterinsurgency campaign since the Coalition presence in Afghanistan began in 2001. Operating in three separate and austere provinces that had been bereft of government efficacy for years, the Brigade constructed expeditionary bases and air fields, and struck decisively at the heart of the Taliban insurgency with Operation KHANJAR in July 2009. Cities and hamlets across the region, from Now Zad to Khan Neshin, resumed regional commerce and schooling for children, and participated in national elections. Concurrent with kinetic fighting, the Brigade engaged tribal, religious, and government leaders with population-centric civil-military operations that synchronized developmental efforts across 58,000 square miles of battle-space. In February 2010, Operation MOSHTARAK reclaimed Marjah, a strategic agricultural hub and narco-terrorist safe haven in the Helmand River Valley. Together with thousands of Afghan National Security Forces, the Brigade tangibly improved the geo-political landscape of Southwestern Afghanistan.

———————

In 2010, Marines fighting alongside British and Afghan forces launched Operation *Moshtarak* in Helmand province in an effort to clear the Taliban out of the central part of the province. Combat operations intensified during this period, especially in the Marjah District of Helmand province. At the same time, Marines aided in the intensified training that prepared Afghanistan military and police forces to take over security of their nation. In April, I Marine Expeditionary Force (Forward) replaced the 2d Marine Expeditionary Brigade as Regional Command-Southwest.

In September, Afghanistan held parliamentary elections for the Wolesi Jirga (House of the People), but the outcome was clouded by Taliban opposition and internal Afghan government dissension. In November, the North Atlantic Treaty Organization (NATO) announced its plans to end combat operations in Afghanistan in 2014. On November 21, Lance Corporal William Kyle Carpenter saved a fellow Marine in combat in Helmand province's Marjah District, an action for which Carpenter was posthumously awarded the Medal of Honor. Carpenter was serving as an automatic rifleman with Company F, 2d Battalion, 9th Marines, Regimental Combat Team I, 1st Marine Division (Forward), I Marine Expeditionary Force (Forward). The citation reads:

> Lance Corporal Carpenter was a member of a platoon-sized coalition force, comprised of two reinforced Marine rifle squads partnered with an Afghan National Army squad. The platoon had established Patrol Base Dakota two days earlier in a small village in the Marjah District in order to disrupt enemy activity and provide security for the local Afghan population. Lance Corporal Carpenter and a fellow Marine were manning a rooftop security position on the perimeter of Patrol Base Dakota when the enemy initiated a daylight attack with hand grenades, one of which landed inside their sandbagged position. Without hesitation and with complete disregard for his own safety, Lance Corporal Carpenter moved toward the grenade in an attempt to shield his fellow

Marine from the deadly blast. When the grenade detonated, his body absorbed the brunt of the blast, severely wounding him, but saving the life of his fellow Marine.

During 2011, Marine units rotated into Afghanistan and continued to conduct raids and patrols throughout the Marineistan provinces, suppressing the poppy harvest and eliminating Taliban caches and sanctuaries. In March, II Marine Expeditionary Force (Forward) replaced I Marine Expeditionary Force (Forward) as Regional Command-Southwest.

In May 2011, U.S. Navy SEALs raided Osama bin Laden's hiding place in Pakistan, killing the al-Qaeda leader. In June, President Barack Obama announced the end of the Afghanistan surge and the withdrawal of more than 30,000 American troops by the following summer. On July 18, 2011, Marine General John R. Allen took command of the International Security Assistance Force (ISAF) and U.S. Forces Afghanistan (USFOR-A), becoming the senior American commander in Afghanistan.

By January 2012, the Marine Corps' reputation was bruised and the Afghan War effort was set back when video footage emerged of Marines urinating on three Afghan corpses, one of several incidents involving coalition troops that outraged many Afghans and Americans. In February, U.S. Defense Secretary Leon E. Panetta announced the intention to end combat missions in Afghanistan as early as mid-2013 and to assign American troops in an advisory role until their withdrawal in 2014. On March 12, I Marine Expeditionary Force (I MEF-Forward) relieved II MEF (Forward) as RC-Southwest.

Despite the controversies and announced troop drawdowns, throughout 2012, Marine units continued to rotate into Afghanistan and conduct raids and patrols throughout the Marineistan provinces, suppressing the poppy harvest and eliminating Taliban caches and sanctuaries.

In late 2012, the Taliban proved that it was still dangerous when it launched a successful raid on Camp Bastion, an airfield and logistics base north-west of Lashkar Gah, Helmand province. They killed two Marines, destroyed six McDonnell Douglas AV-8B Harrier IIs, and badly damaged two other Harriers from Marine Attack Squadron 211 (VMA-211). The Taliban fighters were all captured or killed in the attack, during which Marine aviation personnel fought as infantry, a role Marines of this squadron last performed on Wake Island during World War II.

Marine General John R. Allen was replaced on February 10, 2013 by Marine General Joseph F. Dunford Jr.

On February 28, II Marine Expeditionary Force (Forward) relieved I Marine Expeditionary Force (Forward) as Regional Command-Southwest (RC-Southwest). Marines continued counterinsurgency and training operations throughout 2014, turning over responsibility for security operations district by district to Afghani forces.

On June 18, NATO handed over operations to the Afghan military. Marines, along with the rest of the American forces still in Afghanistan, focused on training missions.

Marines continued counterinsurgency and training operations throughout 2014. In February, II Marine Expeditionary Force (Forward) turned RC-Southwest over to Marine Expeditionary Brigade-Afghanistan (MEB-A). In April, Afghanistan held presidential elections, followed by a run-off election in June. Ashraf Ghani replaced Hamid Karzai as president of Afghanistan in an historic democratic transfer of power. In May 2014, President Barack H. Obama declared that U.S. combat operations in Afghanistan would end in December of the same year.

On August 26, 2014, U.S. Army General John F. Campbell succeeded General Joseph F. Dunford Jr. as commander of the International Security Assistance Force (ISAF) and U.S. Forces Afghanistan.

In October 2014, Marines handed Camp Leatherneck in Helmand province over to Afghan forces, and in December, NATO and the United States "ended" combat operations in Afghanistan. Unfortunately, this act proved premature. Since

2014, the insurgency in Afghanistan has increased, and the U.S. Army has redeployed major units there. Marines remained in Afghanistan serving in joint operations billets in the training mission. The war in Afghanistan has yet to reach a clean conclusion.

Marines returned to Iraq in 2014 to help with the war against the Islamic State of Iraq and the Levant (commonly known as ISIS) and they returned to Afghanistan in 2018 to aid against the resurgent Taleban. But today the focus has shifted to the Pacific region, where the U.S. Navy and the Marine Corps are planning ways to counter the threat China poses in the South China Sea.

Over 240 years after it was founded, the Marine Corps' value as the nation's premier expeditionary force is greater than ever. The Corps continues to develop new expeditionary weapons and works to integrate itself with U.S. Navy maritime strategic doctrine.

Since 1775 Marines have served the United States, providing an expeditionary force capable of projecting power overseas in support of American interests and objectives. It is a unique military organization, providing the nation with unique capabilities. The Marine Corps' motto is *Semper Fidelis*, and the Corps shows no signs of ever betraying that pledge.

SOURCES

Heinl, Robert D. *Soldiers of the Sea: The United States Marine Corps, 1775-1962* (Annapolis: United States Naval Institute, 1962)

Metcalf, Clyde Hill. *A History of the United States Marine Corps* (New York: G. Putnam's Sons, 1939)

Millett, Allan R. *Semper Fidelis: The History of the United States Marine Corps,* Revised and Expanded Edition (New York, 1991)

Neimeyer, Charles P. (ed.) *On the Corps: USMC Wisdom from the Pages of Leatherneck, Marine Corps Gazette, and Proceedings* (Annapolis: Naval Institute Press, 2008)

O'Connell, Aaron. *Underdogs: The Making of the Modern Marine Corps* (Cambridge: Harvard University Press, 2012)

Simmons, Edwin H. *The United States Marine: A History* (Annapolis: Naval Institute Press, 2002)

Westermeyer, Paul W. *The Legacy of Belleau Wood: 100 Years of Making Marines and Winning Battles* (Quantico: Marine Corps History Division, 2018)

ACKNOWLEDGEMENTS

Any errors, omissions, or mistakes within this work are my own, but such a work would not be possible without the support I have received over the years from mentors and colleagues in Marine and military history. I'd like to thank my mentors, Dr. John F. Guilmartin, Charles D. Melson, Dr. Alan R. Millett, and Charles R. Smith. And I would also like to thank my colleagues, Douglas Nash, Dr. Breanne Robertson Chen, Annette Amerman, and Dr. Nicholas Schlosser.

Finally, this work would not have been possible without the patience of my family, Kelly, Tori, and Ren.

INDEX